Gold, Jade and Elegance

By
HELEN B. RAND

"The discovery of Gold proved to be a major incentive to the settlement and progress of Oregon."

Original 1974 Text by Helen B. Rand
Revised 2014 by *The Country Side Press*, North Powder, Oregon
Photos courtesy Baker County Library Historic Photo Collection
Baker City, Oregon

Gold, Jade and Elegance

This book includes the complete text of the original *Jade, Gold and Elegance*, 1974 edition. Some photos have been changed/added to represent the era and for picture clarity, there are also some corrections of typographical errors and regularization of punctuation. Editorial comments are in brackets [ ].

Printing History
Original edition printed in 1974 by *The Record-Courier*
Revised edition printed 2014 by *The Country Side Press*

All Rights Reserved.
Original copyright © by Helen B. Rand
Copyright © 2014 by The Country Side Press/Debby Schoeningh

No part of this book may be reproduced in any form by any electronic or mechanical means (including photocoying, recording, or information storage and retrieval) without permission in writing from the publisher.

Published by *The Country Side Press*, North Powder, OR 97867

Book Design and Layout by Joni Lea Linscott
Typesetting by Sandy Harper
Cover Design and Proofreading by Debby Schoeningh/The Country Side Press
Cover photos: Auburn Blacksmith Shop; Emeline McCallum Hazeltine, wife of George "Irving" Hazeltine and grandmother of author, Helen Biggs Rand

Photos courtesty Baker County Library Historic Photo Collection

ISBN-10: 0-9746360-9-6
ISBN-13: 978-0-9746360-9-2

Library of Congress Control Number: 2014947182

TABLE OF CONTENTS

PART ONE
1862-1870

Gold! And Then The Oregon Settlers Stayed 1
"The Laws Were Nailed to the Trees" Life in the Mining Camps 7
Olds' Ferry Did a "Land Office Business" 19
Rendezvous Trouble at Washoe Ferry 23
Peter Skene Ogden: The Fur Trader Preceded The Great Migration .. 25
Local Place Names and Their Origin 29
Pocahontas, The Town Named for an Indian Princess 35
Joaquin Miller and the Canyon City Literary Society 39

PART TWO

Gold or Jade? The Chinese in the Mining Area 45

PART THREE

The Second Gold Rush: 1890-1914

Days of Elegance 59
Some Old Houses and the People Who Lived in Them 67
The Gold City on the Opera Circuit 75
Alpha Club and the Baker Public Library 81
The Warshauer and the Geiser Grand 87
Stuffy Air and Cinders: The Sumpter Valley Railway 91

Chinese Symbol translates in English to "jade."

PREFACE

These accounts are as authentic as possible after a lapse of one hundred years. The grandparents and many of their contemporaries lived well into our adult lives, talking, writing and being interviewed over and over. They saved letters and newspapers of the eighteen-sixties and seventies.

The grandfathers were not just miners. W. H. Packwood was the last surviving member of the Oregon Constitutional Convention. G. I. Hazeltine and his brother, Martin, were well-known photographers of the early West.

The in-between generation gave us memories and information.

The stories of the nineteen-hundreds are based mainly on my own recollections and those of several old friends. Many thanks for their help.

My husband supplied suggestions, criticism and some commas and colons.

Helen B. Rand

PART ONE
1862-1870

Gold! And Then
The Oregon Settlers Stayed

One of the odd quirks of history is the fact that situations so well known to one generation are soon forgotten, overlooked or never known to later generations. A good example of this is the discovery of gold in the Inland Empire (Eastern Oregon, Eastern Washington and Idaho) which proved to be a major incentive to the settlement and progress of Oregon as a whole during the decade from 1860 to 1870. The importance of this fact seems not to be generally known today.

Over the years there were many travelers through the great interior after the first overland journey by a company led by Wilson Price Hunt for John Jacob Astor in search of furs. This company followed the Snake River through Idaho; and being the first to come overland made the great mistake of staying with the great river as it made its way through the mountains and eventually attempted unsuccessfully to go through what is now known as Hell's Canyon. Their sufferings were great and consequently later parties turned off at Farewell Bend, moved through the Powder River and Grande Ronde valleys, over the Blue Mountains and thence to the Columbia River.

Following this party were the trappers of the Hudson's Bay Company which had received its charter to work in Oregon and Washington territories in 1821. Peter Skene Ogden and others followed up the Deschutes, then eastward and down Burnt River to the Snake and trapped back and forth through Oregon and Idaho.

There were other expeditions by Americans, one by Captain Bonneville, who came as far as Walla Walla in 1832. Then came Captain Nathaniel Wyeth on his first expedition in 1832. On his trip he was accompanied by Jason Lee and other Methodist missionaries on their way to the Willamette.

In 1836 the Presbyterians sent Marcus Whitman, his wife Narcissa, and the Rev. H. H. Spalding and his wife, to start a mission near Walla Walla, called Wailatpu. This location had been chosen the year before by the Rev. Samuel Parker.

The Influence of Gold in the Settlement of Oregon

Beginning in 1842 trains of settlers began to follow the Oregon Trail. But none of these emigrants, trappers or missionaries settled in Eastern Oregon. It took the miners to bring the first permanent settlers.

The settlements along the Willamette River struggled along, making no great gains in population. Leslie Scott, Oregon historian, has said that early progress in Oregon proceeded at "ox wagon speed" and Oregon was a "district proverbial for retarded growth."

Meanwhile value of gold production reached its peak in California in 1851 and by 1855 had dropped more than $20,000,000 due to exhaustion of the easy pickings. A search for new gold-rich districts was rapid and widespread. One of the first major discoveries was made in British Columbia. Not only miners but carpenters, merchants and laborers of all kinds rushed from California to Victoria. It took all the available ships to carry them north and many could get passage only to Portland with the hope that other ways could be found to get them to the new camps. Fares from San Francisco to Portland were $30 for the "roughs" and $60 for the "nobs." Supplies were bought in Portland and this gave local trade a big lift.

Miners Venture Inland

Due to Indian troubles, General Wool, then Commander of the Dept. of the Pacific at Fort Vancouver, had discouraged settlement east of the Cascades, but he had accepted miners because the Indians considered them to be too temporary and not likely to preempt their lands. Poor Indians! Little did they know.

Two parties prospected in Eastern Oregon in the Summer and Fall of 1861. Both were in search of the stream where the so-called Blue Bucket strike had been found. One group contained the men who discovered gold in Griffin Gulch.

Another party prospecting along the John Day River was set upon by Indians who killed all but two of their group. These two made their way back to The Dalles and told of finding gold.

The Auburn group had gone to Walla Walla for supplies and there the word spread. Joined with this news came a much greater piece of news. It was the word of the big strike in the Idaho country at Oro Fino and Salmon River. This news reached California. In the following Spring (1862) the miners burst into the Inland Empire, almost it seemed, by spontaneous combustion. Some came from the Willamette Valley and others from California by the overland route.

The rapidity with which news of a new mining strike spread in a remote wilderness never fails to astonish us. Merchants, farmers and workers of all kinds followed the miners and as always saloons and "hurdy gurdy" houses appeared as if by clairvoyance and soon were running full blast. Settlers in wagon trains came along, and finding people already there, stayed to make their homes.

The "Mother" Camps

William H. Packwood called Auburn the "mother of mining camps" in Baker County and this was true also of Canyon City in Grant County. From these bases men fanned out in all directions looking for "color." They explored streams, mountains and sage-covered hills. They penetrated into locations which seem almost inaccessible today, dependent as we are on the gasoline engine. Some had horses but others were on foot. Practically every inch of the Blue Mountains was explored in the first few weeks. Mr. Hazeltine in Canyon City said, "Men are coming and going in all directions."

By 1870 the first boom was over. But it had served its purpose. Eastern Oregon, Idaho and Montana had permanent settlements. The founding of Boise and Lewiston in Idaho, Baker in Eastern Oregon, and Helena in Montana, and many other towns and cities, was the direct result of the gold rush. An additional benefit was that the railroads came in sooner than they would have done otherwise.

As for Portland, the impetus created by the search for gold carried this city forward toward the metropolis it now is. By 1867 the total production of gold in Oregon since 1862 was $20,000,000. But Portland was also the receiving station for gold from other fields. During the same period Idaho produced $45,000,000 Montana $65,000,000 and Washington $10,000,000. Even this does not tell the whole story as it applies only to gold on its way to the mint. Surely as much gold again must have gone for supplies, food, investment in land, livestock and other materials and services needed by the miners, to say nothing about what was lost in gambling and saloons.

Probably the greatest sources of wealth to early-day Portland came from the proceeds of Oregon Steam Navigation Company. This company was organized to handle transportation and trade to the Inland Empire. It had a monopoly on Columbia River travel and some of the solid fortunes of Portland were founded on the proceeds of its operation. Money was also made by packers and stage coach companies.

At the present in these early years of the 1970's there is a new interest in gold due to its high price on the world's market. There is still gold in Oregon and old mines may be opened and new discoveries made. If this happens, rest assured, gold mining once again will work to the benefit of the State.

(Parts of this article have been excerpted from the author's article of May, 1959 in the Ore Bin, publication of Oregon Dept. of Geology and Minerals Industries.)

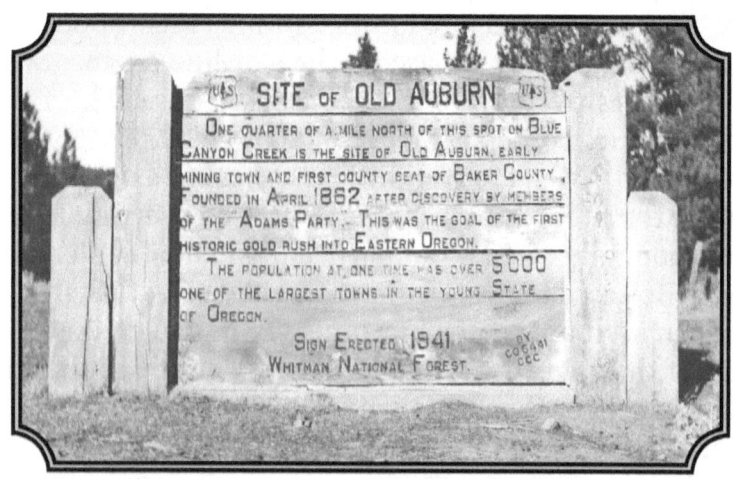

Auburn, Oregon, town site sign. Erected in 1941 by Co. 6441 of the Citizen Conservation Corps.

"This is a photograh of a part of upper Auburn taken from near my office. Freeze Out Gulch mining ground lays near and the hill beyond lays between Blue Canon and Freeze Out. There is a little snow on the ground in this picture."

Picture, believed identified on its back by Samuel Clark, first County Clerk of Baker County, was preserved by Edith Packwood Rand.

William H. Packwood & Johanna O'Brien Packwood

Hunt Mountain

Photo by Bow Lynne McEwen

Nea, Viola, and Gracia Hazeltine, daughters of M. M. Hazeltine.

"The Laws Were Nailed to the Trees"
Life in the Mining Camps

Oswald West, late Governor of Oregon and historian, once wrote, "Life in the Oregon mining camps was drab." While his meaning is clear it seems that "drab" is hardly the word. Life was never drab when fortune always lay under the next turn of the shovel or swish of the gold pan. But compared to the first rush to California life was comparatively uneventful. The gold rush in 1849 was the first in the United States and stirred the country from the Pacific to the Atlantic. Men came from everywhere, not only from the states. They came from Britain, Germany, France, Australia and even China. It was wild and exciting. Most of the participants were amateurs, accompanied by adventures of all kinds.

By the time gold was discovered in Oregon and Idaho the searchers were practically professionals in looking for gold, many experienced in California and Nevada. Life in the Camps took a different turn.

Of course, they were young and adventurous. These were no white-bearded prospectors with burros, as so often pictured. It took the young and healthy to explore the wilderness. But they had been trained in mining procedure and organization of a new camp.

What they came to in Oregon was the expanse of the Blue Mountains, covering most of what is now Baker and Grant counties. They made many strikes, and camps grew up around them. In the Auburn district and surroundings there were Pocahontas, Washington Gulch, Malheur City, Eldorado, Sparta, to name a few; and in Grant county, Marysville, Prairie Diggings, Granite and others. But this section will be concerned with the most important ones, Auburn and Canon Creek. The original spelling of this creek and town and also Blue Canon at Auburn was due to the Spanish influence of the Californians.

Two Families

Much of the information for this chapter has been taken from the letters, records and recollections of two families, William H. Packwood and his wife, Joanna, in Auburn and George Irving Hazeltine and his wife, Emeline, in Canon City. William was 30 and Joanna 20 in 1862. Packwood had come from mining in Southern Oregon and Joanna O'Brien had accompanied her sister and brother-in-law from Iowa to help care for their baby. She did not intend to stay but was soon called to be Auburn's first school teacher. After six weeks she was married to Packwood and had to give up the school as teachers were not allowed to be married. They spent the rest of their long lives in Baker County.

Irving Hazeltine and his brother-in-law, Van Middlesworth, came from California with the first Californians, having left their wives with their parents. They planned to make a strike and return home at the end of the summer. They stayed a year. In 1862 Irving was 26 and Emeline 19. They, their wives and wives' families also spent the rest of their long lives in Canon City and John Day.

Auburn and Canon City developed in somewhat different ways. Auburn, since it was on the emigrant path to the Willamette Valley, attracted many home seekers and business men, people looking for a place to settle down. It would have continued as a permanent town, perhaps, if Baker City had not been so close. But Baker City had been settled on the edge of a fertile valley with fine farming land. After the mines began to peter out, people simply moved their businesses to Baker City.

Canon City, on the other hand, was considered a place to camp until the gold ran out. The merchants, saloon keeper, etc., came only to serve the miners. The miners had no intention of settling. But when the settlers did come to farm the beautiful John Day Valley, the mining camp was so close that the two settlements became one.

At first they were called Upper and Lower Town, later Canyon City and John Day. They were really almost one town as they actually are today. The mining claims followed the creek south from its confluence with the John Day River. Ironically, while Auburn was found by men looking for the Blue Bucket, Canyon Creek was very probably the location of this famous tale.

"The Laws Were Nailed to the Trees"

While both locations consisted of both Oregonians and Californians, the latter were in the majority and took over the organization of the camps. The first thing to do was to draw up mining laws and elect a Recorder of Claims, the most important office in the camp. The laws were written out and nailed to the trees where all could read them. An account of the first meeting in Canyon City is to be found in the Grant County Courthouse.

A meeting was called on July 19, 1862. Major Howard was in the chair, probably a convenient stump. George Woodman of California was elected Recorder. Twenty nine laws were adopted after first defining the limits of John Day's district.

The first article is as follows: "Each person mining in the district shall be entitled to two claims by location, one in a ravine, hill, gulch, creek or flat as the case may be and one in the river; and one by purchase. Every claim located or purchased shall be represented."

Other articles designated size of claims and time limit for selection. Others recognized the subject of weather. Creek claims would be workable from June 1-Nov. 1 except Canon Creek, which was not workable until July 20. Article 8 says no claim shall be deemed forfeited from November until June 20, 1863. All claims will be forfeited if one day's work on claim in seven is not completed.

Article 19 said: "No person disabled by sickness or absent in any Indian wars shall be deemed to have forfeited his claim by reason of sickness or service."

Article 25 said: "All persons now holding claims in this district shall have seven days to record same from July 5, 1862."

These laws are preserved in the Grant County Courthouse and undoubtedly were similar in other districts.

Lay Out Of Auburn Town

In Auburn a group containing Wm. Packwood, George Hall, Ed. Cranston, John Bowen and others decided to lay out a town in June 1862. It was to be called Auburn and a street was located. A miner's meeting was called to elect the important Recorder. E. C. Brainard and Packwood were the candidates. They voted in a primitive but practical way by asking the followers of each candidate to form on two sides of a log. It was not a secret ballot but it worked. Brainard was elected. From June 23, 1862, to May 6, 1863, he recorded 1,291 claims in Blue Canon district. George Hall was elected the first Sheriff, the second most important office.

The people first lived in tents, of course, but soon log houses were going up. The oldest picture around of Auburn shows several log houses built on short stilts to allow for the deep snow. Later there were some of sawed lumber. Hazeltine and Middlesworth built a house in the spring of 1863 at Canon. They had decided to bring their wives to Eastern Oregon. They hired a man named Hudson to work on it and leave them free to mine. Mr. Hudson was paid $37 for hewing logs and five days work on the house. When it was completed it had cost $350, and was the best on the creek. The owners continued to live in it but also rented it to Mr. Dye's son for a store. The older Mr. Dye had come in the summer of 1862 with merchandise and driving a herd of cattle to sell for beef.

After a time the merchant began to miss dried fruits. He accused the owners of stealing. Incensed, they ordered him to move out. When he took down some high boots hanging on the wall the fruits fell out. They had been hidden there by packrats.

People and Life in The Camps

The early miners worked in companies. There were not enough good claims to go around so they formed partnerships. Men who had no claims worked for the others as day laborers.

There were several men in the early days of Auburn who became prominent in Oregon. One was Thomas McBride, who became Chief Justice of the Oregon Supreme Court. Another, Judge McArthur, whose son Lewis A. McArthur was the author of *Oregon Geographic Names*.

The Idaho World, printed in Idaho City, reported in 1865 that Henry Comstock was in John Day in 1865 and had struck a quartz lead and the *San Francisco Daily Bulletin* said that he was in Auburn at Christmas, 1863. He also mined in Idaho and Montana but his intellect had darkened and he imagined that he was back in Nevada where he had been considered to be the discoverer of the great lode that bore his name. In 1870 he shot himself in Bozeman and was found without a cent in his pocket. (*Anaconda Standard*)

Back in the thirties when I first read about the prices of food I was shocked. I am no longer. It is worse now and our money isn't as good either.

Beef was the least expensive as it was brought in on the hoof and butchered on the spot. It usually cost 25¢ a pound. Fifty-pounds of flour sold for $20. In the first year, 100-pounds of "spuds" were $16 but the wonder is that they were available at all. Onions were $1, sugar $2. Sugar and coffee were listed as very scarce.

It is supposed today that game and fish were plentiful; but the fact is that the busy miners had little time to hunt and fish although they occasionally had a deer and sometimes a bear. A bear was welcome because of the large amount of fat. Bear fat made fine huckleberry pie. There were birds also, grouse and sage hen, which have almost disappeared today. Fish were plentiful but fishing took time and had to be found farther afield as the mining disturbed the water in the steams.

Articles besides food had to be purchased too. Matches were 12¢, horse nails 50¢, gloves $2.50 and when it got cold a comforter was $2. A luxury was "segars" and whiskey for $5.75 and tobacco for 50¢. The miner's accounts listed medicine and quite a few items were listed simply as charity. Canned goods were the most expensive but there was sometimes a can of tomatoes for 75¢. Dried fruit was always at hand and a fine mock apple pie could be made of soda crackers, sugar and vinegar.

When the wives and daughters arrived in the camp almost all of them took in boarders, a boon for the single men and extra money for the women. In 1863, when Emeline and Christy came to join their husbands, their parents, three sisters and little brother came along to make their home in John Day. At once, Mrs. McCollum insisted on a cooking stove. It was shipped in from The Dalles, having originally come around the Horn. It came in pieces to be set up. What a treasure it was. A boarding house was set up as soon as it came.

Another use for the stove was to heat the flat irons for ironing clothes. Emeline remembered that Irving used to roast a pan of coffee in the oven on her ironing day. Another use was to dry the pans of gold dust under the stove.

All freight and mail came to John Day from The Dalles. How the lonesome men waited for the mail. Emeline said that mail call began at the river and passed from man to man along the creek for miles.

There is not much record of churches in accounts of the early days. One says that a little church burned down in Auburn in 1864. No other information.

Ellen McCallum told us that as a girl of fourteen in Canyon City and John Day she accompanied the Sheriff's wife around the towns to collect money to build a church. An accommodating man made the rounds of the saloons for them and in one day they had enough gold dust to build the church.

Residents Were Respectable Citizens

"Paint Your Wagon" and its like are great fun; but sometimes we must tell it like it was. To use a modern expression, there were two lifestyles in the mining camp, side by side, but with no communication, among the women at least.

As soon as the big strikes were made the saloons and prostitutes came in. They were welcomed by the lonesome miners who were far from home and family. The men worked hard every day and needed some relaxation at night. The house and dance halls provided all the entertainment there was. And they were young and living in an invigorating mountain atmosphere. So the drinking and gambling went on every night and many times men lost all they had worked so hard for all day.

But what is not often realized today is that there were many respectable women also. They came in with their fathers and husbands. There were children, too. Almost the first thing they did in Auburn was to organize a school. Mr. Hazeltine wrote to this bride, "There are several nice women here. You will not lack for company."

The "Hurdy Gurdy" houses were often just dance halls. William Trimble in his "Mining Advance into the Inland Empire" said, "It is a mistake to confuse these dance halls with houses of prostitution; seldom did one of these women become a prostitute and some of them settled down in the community and became good wives. A very respected miner told me that he knows a number of these women and had been acquainted with their later careers and that all had turned out well."

During the winter of 1863 word came into Canyon City that a

group of German girls were being brought in to become wives of the miners and they excitedly prepared to receive them. Irving Hazeltine was a fiddler and a good dancer so a group of men came to him and asked him to teach them how to dance. He wrote home about these:

Dancing School for Miners

"It is now quite late in the night and I have just returned from my dancing school. I have twenty-eight scholars and the most of them are very clumsy and awkward and you know, I am obliged to dance with all of them to give them the right step and motion and I can tell you it is no boy's play. Once in a while one of those 'web-footed' Oregonians, weighing about two hundred would jump about two feet and come down with their heels on my toes and I could hardly keep from screaming with pain. But they are learning fast and I shall soon have them quiet and easy dancers. It is much like taming a wild cayuse, though and if you could see them bucking around trying to dance and Highland Schottische you would be forcibly reminded of some unruly animal of the mule species performing under the pressure of the first saddle.

"I have now twenty-eight scholars, at eight dollars per scholar for a term of twelve lessons. After paying for the room, lights and music in fact after all expenses are paid I shall make about one hundred dollars. That is what I teach dancing school for."

In his next letter he wrote:

"You ask the reason why I do not teach young ladies how to dance. First, I would not get any more pay for teaching them than for the men alone. Second, if I taught ladies I could not do it with a grey shirt on and of necessity I would have been obliged to buy a fine suit of clothes which would have taken all my one hundred dollars. I would have been out my boot leather and fiddle strings for nothing. Third, there is but one young lady in camp and the ladies that wanted to learn here are all older than I am, such as Mrs. Winklepaw, Mrs. Toothache, etc. (these are real names) all of them over thirty-five; and last but not least, I do not care a fig to be in other ladies' society since I met you."

The school was taught from a little book which is still in existence. It was published in 1855 and is called *Ferrero's Art of Dancing and Ball Room Instruction.* Dances and Quadrilles, Mazurkas, waltzes, etc. and the second half of the book contains the music for them.

The German girls came in and became part of the community. One of them married a man who became one of the leading citizens of the state.

In The Early Canyon Camp

Some records have been kept of the signs of the early mining camps.

One sign on the Canyon City Street was this one:

> **NUGGET SALOON**
> **Best grade of wines and liquors served at the bar**
> **John Clayton, Prop.**
> **Women and minors not allowed**

Another sign:

> **WHISKEY GULCH SALOON**
> **Canyon City 1862**
> **Hurdy gurdy, dancing and gambling**
> **No bet too big to call**
> **Bring your poke and ante**
> **Shod horses must be rode up to the rear**

The most famous madam of the time was Mary St. Clair. Her establishment went on for so long that her will is preserved in the Grant County Courthouse.

A letter written in the Spring of 1863 described a night at St. Clair's. It was from Tom Fawcett, on the creek at the time. He said, "I understand they had quite a row at old Mary's last night. A theater performance took off some of the characters in the camp. It pinched rather heavy in some quarters and friends of the parties undertook to break up the whole thing. The consequence was a general row in which pistols and knives flourished and oaths was shot off until you couldn't rest. Nobody hurt except those that drank whiskey and fell among the rubble chopped to pieces by the city defenders. All is quiet today.

Panorama of Baker City from Old Reservoir Hill. In foreground is a baseball park located between East and Ash, Auburn and Spring Garden streets.

"Another happening was that Bill Broadwater had a fight with a big Dutchman — casualties, several black eyes, swelled noses and sore ribs and the destruction of a lot of good whiskey."

The last item in this letter told of the most famous murder in this camp.

"You doubtless heard of the murder of Galiger, the packer, by Berry Way. He got away from the Sheriff and that's the last of him. His wife is here and a sweet specimen of feminine modesty she is, too. She can let out any old Blister you ever saw – gets drunk, rips and tears about in beautiful style. The Sheriff locked her up one night and now she is sulking about looking for a chance to shoot him."

When the Stable was the Depot.

Columbia Mine crew posed before mine entrance with two tracks emerging.

Parade on Main Street in Baker City. There appears to be a bird with a long tail on top of the pole on the buggy.

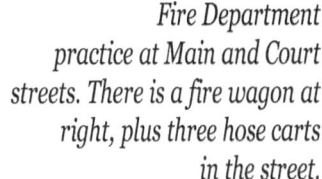

Fire Department practice at Main and Court streets. There is a fire wagon at right, plus three hose carts in the street.

Stagecoach in front of old high school. [W.H. and Johanna Packwood are probably the persons sitting in the coach.]

Played Solitaire on His Own Coffin

Berry Way was afterwards caught and hanged. One of the early badmen in John Day rode to his hanging on his own coffin playing solitaire as he rode. This was perhaps Berry Way.

There were deaths in the camps but they were not all shootings. Some were the result of pneumonia, accidents or blood poisoning always a vicious killer at that time. Judge Fred Wilson of The Dalles told a story that might or might not be true, but the Judge was a good historian. He said:

"The early miners were so busy that they had little time for burying. They hired one fellow to take care of this. He found a nice flat spot on the hill above the creek for a cemetery. He made the coffins, dug the graves and interred the remains. After some time parents of a young man who had died came in with a wagon to get the body to take home for re-burial. The custodian took them to the cemetery, showed them the graves and said, "Leave the ones on this side," waved his arm and pointed to the others and said, "Take your choice." They were all un-marked.

The wild life did not last very long in either camp. More and more settlers came in and there were many more amusements, amateur theatricals, dances, some attempt at culture. Also, in good weather, bonfires where everyone sat around the fire and sang the songs of the Civil War. Some of the songs mentioned were "Crankadillo" and "Passing Away Tonight."

Olds' Ferry near Farewell Bend. The automobile on the ferry dates the photo to around 1915. The ferry was used until 1920, when it was taken to Brownlee and used several years by a sheep operation.

Olds' Ferry
Did a "Land Office Business"

For the last three of four years recreationists have enjoyed the new park at Farewell Bend. They have camped, fished and boated at this beautiful spot. How many of these people have stopped to think of how it was one hundred years ago?

Since the 1830s this had been an important location on the Oregon Trail. It was the crossing for the emigrants leaving the river behind. On reaching the Oregon side they made their way up the hill and down to the site of the present town of Huntington. Some years ago the ruts of these wagons could still be seen on the flat top of the hill and can still be identified by a discerning observer.

There were three primitive ferries on this stretch of the Snake, one the Washoe at the mouth of the Malheur, next the Central at the mouth of the Weiser and last, the Olds at Farewell Bend. All three were used but most of the travelers stayed on the Idaho side until they came to the big bend.

The first ferry at the bend was just a raft but about 1859 a better ferry was built by J. P. Olds, then an employee of the Hudson's Bay Company which still had a few trappers in the country. With difficulty logs were floated down the Burnt River which enters the Snake near this point. The logs were made into a boat with the primitive tools available to the people at that time. The first cable used by the owners was brought to Oregon around the Horn.

In 1859 the only major road east of the Cascades was from Fort Boise, Idaho, to Walla Walla, Washington. The Overland stage route from Kelton, Nevada, entered Oregon near Fort Boise and continued north on the main road northwest to Umatilla landing, then westward to The Dalles, becoming the Northwest Stage route after joining the Walla Walla road. The Olds' ferry served the wants of the stage and other travelers. It was a famous station during the rush to the gold mines in 1862. It was an example of the many obstacles overcome by the pioneers in opening the West.

Ferry Fees of Record

The district in which the ferry was situated in 1864 was part of Baker County. There is on record an order of the county court dated March 7, 1865, granting Olds a license for a ferry at Farewell Bend, tolls of which were to be the same as those charged by the Boise ferry. The schedule of charges was fixed at 25¢ for footmen, 50¢ for pack animals, 25¢ for loose animals, $2 for a wagon, two horses and a ton of freight with $1 additional for each ton of freight.

Later on July 4, 1867, the ferry fees at Olds amounted to over $1,000. The charges for a four-horse team, $3; two-horse team, $2.50; single horse or cow 50¢. The boats at that time were from 50 to 60 feet long and about 15 feet wide. They were at first operated with six men at the oars. Later on wire cables were stretched across the river in which the boats were anchored by means of which they were pulled across the channel taking from seven to eight minutes. In 1867 a steamboat was built and plied between Olds' and Glenn's ferries, a distance of 135 miles.

Several years later trouble started when Burnt River toll road and

Olds' ferry consolidated their interests under the name of Burnt River Toll Road, Bridge and Ferry Company. Memories of old hardships were forgotten and newcomers objected on principle to paying tolls. A good deal of money was expended on maintaining the road and ferry although the word "bridge" in the company title was never anything but an aspiration. The ferry was not always a money-maker and profits of boom years were seldom available to cover the lean ones.

In 1865 W. H. Packwood joined Olds and a man named Parsons and incorporated a company combining Olds, Central and Washoe ferries. Olds was President of the company and Packwood Secretary and Treasurer. Packwood was in the operation until he left to build the Eldorado Ditch.

At this time the ferry did a land office business, for the Idaho gravel mines had been struck at Idaho City and the road was a procession of hurrying humanity on foot, horseback and team to reach the coveted goal. Huge pack trains were carrying in freight for the stores to be established and mammoth freight teams driven by "jerk" lines were moving along daily.

Woman's Written Account Preserved

After purchasing the ferries Mr. and Mrs. Packwood left Auburn with their little daughter Molly, who had been the first white child born in Auburn. Mrs. Packwood left a written account of the trip and of her life at the ferry:

"In short order we prepared to leave for Olds' Ferry, myself, baby and Mr. Packwood. Our outfit consisted of a rickety spring wagon and two horses with rope harness. I prepared provisions for the trip and we got stalled in the mud and slept in the wagon the first night. We had five dollars which we paid Mr. Jackson to haul us out of the mud. The high waters washed the bridges out so I stayed at Straw ranch which was then kept by Mr. and Mrs. Casey.

"I remained about six weeks before being able to continue the journey. So on I went to the ferry. A more dreary place on the Idaho side of the river couldn't be imagined and there my son William was born on the 7th of November, 1865. The ice broke up in January washing out abutments, etc., so we moved to the Oregon side of Snake R.

"Soon after moving the men built an adobe room 16 x 20, fireproof, as the Indians were getting very troublesome. I used the place for a bedroom. It had port holes on both sides, an underground cellar with provisions and ammunition. I had a big Newfoundland dog and many times was alone as the men were crossing stages on the ferry boat.

Escaped Scott Massacre

"It was during this time that Scott and wife were killed by the Indians. Mr. Scott brought us vegetables and had I sufficient bread baked would have been with them as I had promised to go to a dance at Rye Valley with them. I went over when they were killed taking what things I knew would be needed and stayed until they were buried.

"On my return to the ferry I was so nervous, I could not keep quiet so I did quite a washing and just as I was finishing a man named Folger rode up in front of the kitchen window, could not talk held up his coat, showed where he was shot same as Scott and wife. The men were crossing on ferry boat. I ran down to the bank almost crazy and the men came as soon as possible.

"I was so overworked as I cooked for the company's men and I was on the verge of prostration. In addition to my work I kept a sale counter where I sold bread, cake, pies, milk, butter, chickens and eggs and made good money. I kept enough of what I earned to defray my expenses. As the receipts at the ferry often reached $1,000 a day Spring and Fall for many months, I decided to go to Walla Walla for a rest. I talked to the Sisters of Providence to let me board and room with them and again take my music and to enjoy a little refined surroundings once again. Soon after, my husband came to the Convent and told me he had sold the ferry and we were moving to Eldorado."

Rendezvous Trouble at Washoe Ferry
(Based on recollections of W. H. and Joanna Packwood)

When Olds, Packwood and Parsons bought the three ferries on the Snake River – Olds', Central and Washoe Ferries – the purchase was due to trouble on the Washoe ferry. This ferry was at the mouth of the Malheur River. On a 1900 railroad map of this area is found a town of Washoe at that location.

At some time prior to taking on the ferries Mr. Packwood ran a store at Auburn. One night he was called from bed by a young man of about 22 who told him he wanted some meat. He said he was penniless and had walked from California to that place and had not had any meat for three months. Packwood gave him a shoulder of bacon and told him if he ever had any money he could come back and pay. The man's name was Stewart and he afterwards came back and paid. He mined a while and afterwards bought the Washoe ferry with a man named Bryan.

Alex Stewart and Bryan seemed to be honest men; but unfortunately Stewart had a brother who was a notorious character. The Washoe ferry soon became a rendezvous of an organized band of horse thieves. In order to break up the band an Idaho vigilante committee captured Stewart and Bryan, took them up the Payette River and locked them in a one-room cabin, intending to give them a vigilante trial and hang them in the morning. However, Bryan was a locksmith, got hold of a nail and picked the lock during the night and the two men made their escape into Oregon by swimming the river in the chilly month of February.

Stewart made his way to Auburn and told his tale to Packwood. Mrs. Packwood tells in her recollections:

"Alex Stewart came to Auburn to tell his grievances. Stewart's brother had got in trouble with the settlers in that locality. So he wanted to turn over his interests to us to protect him. Accordingly, my husband took Jack Ingraham, who was sheriff, and went to

Washoe ferry and took possession of the ferry and the grand finale was the consolidation of the three ferries, Olds', Central and Washoe."

Stewart told Packwood the ferry was his, to take it and do the best he could with it and if he made anything out of it he could pay Stewart and his partner whatever he thought was right. After legally getting possession of it through sheriff's sale, Packwood paid Stewart and Bryan $5,000. Both Stewart and Bryan were afterward killed.

Ferry Rowed by Oars

As soon as Packwood got possession of the Washoe ferry the horse thief gang was broken up and the three ferries were consolidated under one management. A company was formed and a toll road on Burnt River 35 miles long to the Straw ranch was built. At this time the Washoe was a boat 40 x 60 feet long, had no cable and was manned by six men who rowed the boat across the stream with oars.

During the Indian wars, which he went through here, while the Indians committed many depredations and destroyed much property, none of the ferries were destroyed or any of Packwood's property, not even the stakes on the Eldorado ditch were molested. Packwood did not attribute this to any friendship or respect the Indians had for him or his partners, but accounts for the grade stakes not being disturbed to some superstition the Indians had concerning them.

Mr. Packwood stated that in nine months, from May 15, 1866 to January 16, 1867, the income of these three ferries was $103,000. He stated that in the four years they conducted the ferries, 1865, 1866, 1867 and 1868, they did not lose over $3,000 in bad bills and many times they had considerable more than that amount outstanding on their books.

He cited this to show the honesty of those sturdy pioneers and packers and freighters, who blazed the trail for civilization. They trusted many men packing into the mines whom they had never seen before and they invariably returned and settled their accounts.

Peter Skene Ogden, a Chief Fur Trader with the Hudson's Bay Company.

Peter Skene Ogden: The Fur Trader Preceded the Great Migration

The name of Peter Skene Ogden comes up so often in any account of early Oregon that it is time to put his story into this series because it documents the presence of the fur trader in this section before the great migration.

Peter Skene Ogden was born in Quebec in 1794, the son of Chief Justice Ogden. His godfather, Andrew Skene, was also a judge. Judge Ogden had gone to Canada from the American colonies during the Revolution because he was a Loyalist.

In 1811 when Peter was seventeen years old he secured a position with the Northwest Company. Before this he had worked for a short time for John Jacob Astor in the fur trade. For some years he worked as a clerk in Isle de la Crosse at the lake of the same name in southern Athabasca. While stationed there he married a woman of the Cree tribe and his first son was born at the Fort there in 1817. This son, when grown, entered the service of the Hudson's Bay Company and worked for them until 1870.

When Ogden was 24 he came down the Columbia to Astoria and for some time was in charge of trapping parties operating between the Columbia and Puget Sound. His second son was born in 1819. In 1820 Ogden secured an interest in the Northwest Company and in 1821 the Northwest and Hudson's Bay Company merged. In 1824 Ogden was appointed Chief Trader. From then on his life was full of adventure.

He traveled all over the West, exploring new territory, becoming acquainted with most of the Indian Chiefs in the Oregon country as well as in Northern California and Alaska. His friendship with the Indians made him very valuable in establishing posts and concluding negotiations with the tribes

While Peter Ogden named many places in Oregon, including several in Eastern Oregon, his own name remains only in Utah of which state he was one of the first white men to explore.

His name was given to the city of Ogden and to other minor locations in the same state. He also was the first to find the river now known as the Humboldt. He kept careful journals which have become treasures in the history of the West.

Rescued Whitman Survivors

One of the most important things that he did was to rescue by ransom the people who had been captured by the Indians after the Whitman massacre. When word was received at Fort Vancouver of this tragedy Ogden started out immediately for Walla Walla. On December 24, 1847 he assembled the Indians in Council. He made a speech saying in part:

"We have been among you for 30 years without shedding blood. The Americans, while not of the same nation, are of the same blood, speak the same language and worship the same God as we do. Why can't you control your young men? Besides this butchery you have robbed travelers passing through this country and insulted their women. If you allow your young to govern you, you are not men. If the Americans begin war they will not rest until every one of you is wiped from the earth... Deliver me the prisoners to return to their friends and I will pay you ransom; that is all."

He was answered by Chief Tiloukaikt of the Cayuses: "Chief, your words are weighty and your hairs are gray. We have known you a long time. You have had an unpleasant journey to this place. I cannot therefore keep the families back. I give them back to you which I would not do to another younger than yourself."

On the 29th of December, 50 captives, many of them children, were delivered to Ogden. For these Ogden paid five blankets, fifty shirts, ten fathoms of tobacco, ten handkerchiefs, ten guns and 100 rounds of ammunition.

On New Years Day, 1848 The Reverent H. H. Spalding with ten others arrived at Walla Walla fort from Wailatpu under escort of fifty Nez Perce Indians. These Indians were paid twelve blankets, twelve shirts, twelve handkerchiefs, five fathoms of tobacco, two guns, 200 pounds of ammunition and some knives. This payment was made for the safe conduct of the people to Walla Walla.

Fourteen people had been killed in the massacre including Dr. Marcus Whitman and his wife Narcissa.

Many years later one of the survivors was interviewed. She was Mrs. Elizabeth Sager Helm who had been 10 years old at the time of the massacre. She said, "Uncle Peter was a man you could not help liking. He was medium size but heavy for his height. He was a merry, jolly man always full of jokes. After he had bought us from the Indians we started down the Columbia for Fort Vancouver. There were four or five boatloads of us. Mr. Ogden, like many of the Hudson Bay employees, had an Indian wife. He treated her as respectfully as if she were white."

This was probably his second wife, whom he married after the death of his first wife, and who outlived him by many years. She died at the age of 98. She was a member of the Spokane tribe.

Ogden Was Chief Factor

After Dr. John McLoughlin left the Fort to live in Oregon City Peter Ogden was made Chief Factor of the Hudson's Bay Company. He died in Oregon City in 1854 and was buried in Mountain View cemetery in the city. Seventy years later his worth was recognized and a three-ton granite stone was placed on his grave. Money for this was raised by the Oregon Historical Society.

Some information from article by Fred Lockley in *The Oregonian*.

Local Place Names and Their Origin

Much of this information dealing with the names of local places is well known to the older residents of the Baker area but newcomers and young people often ask about it. So to repeat it here provides both authenticity and a new and available source to answer their questions.

The first place names in this region were given by the trappers of the Hudson's Bay Company. They were often found in the journals of Peter Skene Ogden. The rivers were the first named. The Snake did not get its name because it had a twisted course or because of reptiles. It was called the Snake because tribes of Shoshone Indians lived on its banks and this tribe's name translated into Snakes. Later this tribe was usually called the Snakes, by the miners.

The Malheur was named by the French-Canadians trapping with Ogden. They called it River Malheur (the unfortunate river) because goods that had been hidden nearby had been discovered and stolen by Indians. This name was afterward given to the county.

When ships came to Oregon around the Horn they often went by way of the Sandwich Islands, now Hawaii. Sometimes natives of those islands came on to Oregon with the ship. They found work with the trappers. On February 18, 1826, on Ogden's second expedition into the Snake River country he noted in his journal, "reached Sandwich Island river, so called, owing to two of them murdered by Snake Indians in 1819." This river name was shortened to Owyhee (Hawaii spelled as it sounds).

Ogden also christened the Burnt River but it is not certain why he called it that. Perhaps because of burnt trees or burned looking rocks on the banks.

Powder River Was Named Early

The Powder River was first seen by the Wilson Price Hunt expedition. MacArthur thinks it was probably named by Donald Mackenzie. It was thought that the name came from the Chinook jargon words "po-lallie illahe" meaning sandy or powdery ground. Lewis and Clark show Powder River on their maps as Port-pel-lah River. They never came near it but got their information from the Indians.

From an article by the late J. Neilson Barry, written in 1950, we find this comment:

"Powder River was a very peculiar course. I was amazed to see it indicted on the map for Lewis and Clark, although no white man had ever been within a hundred miles of Powder River. Yet that map indicated its peculiar course.

"I have that Indian map, with Clark's manuscript written in it. He used it for the map of the West that had been ordered by the President. It was published in 1814, eight years after the Indians had drawn the map. Yet before it was published 16 groups of Astorians had traveled in that region, with many trips across the Powder River Valley."

Barry wrote that Lewis and Clark had the map drawn for them near Kamiah, Idaho, in 1806, Clark writing the Indian names on the map, which covered the Seven Devils, Wallowas and Blue Mountains, the then most remote part of the whole continent.

The John Day got its name from an incident during the Hunt expedition when John Day and another man became separated from the main party. They were found wandering near the mouth of the John Day after having had all their clothes stolen. They were almost crazy from the experience. The name John Day for the river was first put in writing by Ogden.

There is one point named for Wilson Price Hunt but it received its title in comparatively recent times. J. Neilson Barry, Oregon historian and once rector of the Baker Episcopal Church, and other interested citizens, requested that the name Hunt be given to a peak in the Elkhorn range. In "Astoria" by Washington Irving, Hunt is mentioned as having seen the range northwest of Baker. The United States Board of Geographical Names acceded to this request. Hunt Mountain is the summit of the northeastern spur of the Elkhorn ridge.

There were never many Indians in Baker Valley so this area does not have the Indian names peculiar to other parts of Eastern Oregon. Telocaset was originally called Antelope stage station. When the railroad went through this name was replaced by the Nez Perce word which means "the top or put at the top overlooking a valley."

Of course, there is Pocahontas but that community will require a whole article.

The first time the name Blue Mountains was found in print or rather writing, was in the journals of David Thompson of the Northwest

Company of Montreal August 8, 1811. He said, "Beginning to see the Blue Mountains."

Place Names and the Civil War

Since the settlement of Baker Valley came at the time of the Civil War, place names were influenced by that event. First, Baker City and Baker County were named for Colonel Edward Baker, Senator from Oregon, who was killed at the battle of Ball's Bluff. His story is well told in *The Record-Courier* of October 11, 1973, by W. Joseph O'Connor. The town of Baker was named by R. A. Pierce who secured some land and built a house west of where the Court House now stands. He called the town just Baker but other citizens thought Baker City sounded better and that form was adopted. In 1911 this was changed back to Baker by vote of the people. This is covered more fully in the "100 year History of the Episcopal Church."

Union County and town names are obvious, the town having been named first. Grant County was titled in honor of U. S. Grant, General and U. S. President.

Many Southern Democrats migrated to Oregon. Some of them had been soldiers in the campaigns of Major-General Sterling Price of the Confederate army. The newcomers in Baker were derisively termed by Republicans "The left wing of Price's army." A community of these people near Baker was referred to as Wingville and it keeps that name today. There are also several "Dixies" around the area.

Some miners near the present-day town of Sumpter named their cabin Fort Sumter, because the shelling of the fort started the Civil war. The miners' spelling of the place (adding a "p" in the center of the word) was never corrected and continues in the name of the town, the valley and memories of the Sumpter Valley Railroad. Bourne was started later and named for Jonathan Bourne, Senator from Oregon 1907-1913. He was interested in Oregon mines.

Another version of the name Sumpter is that Sumpter is a common noun meaning pack animal.

[According to Baker City Historian Gary Dielman, the miners called it "Fort Sumter," after the fort in South Carolina that was shelled. Later the "p" was added, because the Postmaster General didn't want it to have the same spelling as Sumter.]

Auburn was apparently chosen arbitrarily just because it was a pretty word. Granite originally was Independence because it was there that gold was found on July 4, 1862. Later it became Granite because of the rocky soil. Whitney was named for C. H. Whitney, pioneer land owner. Tipton was at the summit of the mountains on the Sumpter Valley Railway at an altitude of 5,100 feet.

There is a story about the naming of Bridgeport. In 1862-1863 gold was discovered near Clarks Creek. Supplies were packed from Baker, crossing Burnt River near where Hereford is now. Bridgeport was on the south bank of the river which could not then be forded. A toll road was constructed and was made passable in 1869. A bridge was built and it was decided to call the community Bridgeport.

Huntington was originally Miller Stage Station. The brothers J. B. and J. M. Huntington bought out Miller and gave their name to the place. Durkee was first Express which may have been a station for Wells-Fargo. The Durkee family had a ranch there and the town has been so called ever since.

Judge Israel D. Haines owned land on which the town of Haines is now situated and he started the community.

"Uncle Tom" Keating, a jolly British sailor, was one of the first settlers in the valley of the lower Powder River. The first name of the community was Irwin, later changed to Keating.

Richland was named for the good soil. Halfway has always been the cause of arguments. Halfway to what? Halfway between Baker and Cornucopia, Halfway between Pine and Carson, Halfway between Baker and Brownlee, Halfway between Pine and Cornucopia seems to be correct. Later the Halfway post office was moved and is now much nearer Pine. The original significance has been lost.

Name On A "Top"

Sparta was named for a Dutchman who found gold in the locality. His name was Kooster. Mr. Packwood recounts the change of the names as follows: "As soon as I had determined to build the ditch (Sparta) it became necessary to have a base or starting point for our work. John Furman, old stage man, told me he would put in a stage line as soon as I began operations. In a few days after this, John Furman had his stage ready and on January 8, 1871, I. B. Bowen, Sr., Ed Cranston, C. M. Foster and myself and Furman left Baker to pick out a point which would make a start in building the ditch. We went over to where Sparta now is and surveyed and located lots. The question came up as to what name should be given the new town. Each of us had a name to propose. I remember Mr. Bowen proposed Iberville. Cranson and Foster each had a name; so to decide on a name, it was proposed to make a wooden top with four sides and on each side write a name and spin the top and the name that showed on top when it fell was the town name. We made the top and each wrote the name he wished for the town. I wrote Sparta, the name of my home town in Illinois, and when the top was spun and fell, Sparta was on top."

Joseph A. Wright store in Sparta. This stone building, which still stands, was built in 1872 by brothers Sigmund and Seligmann (aka E. D. Cohn) Heilner, German immigrants, who had come after doing business for a number of years in northern California and southwestern Oregon.

Baldock Slough was named for Wm. Baldock, pioneer of 1862. Rye Valley was named for the native grass.

There are few distinctive street names in Baker. Main was formerly Front St. and there was still one sign left in comparatively recent times. Broadway was first Center but was changed to give Baker a more metropolitan air.

Mt. Hope Cemetery, Denham and Gooding section. The child is Lloyd Denham, ca. age 3 or 4, son of Hugh and Maggie Gooding Denham. The large stone is enscribed with the names of Gooding family members. The white stone at the right edge of the photo is that of Ethel Ester Denham, daughter of Hugh and Maggie, who died of diphtheria at age 7.

    Place street was the Baker end of a toll road built from Auburn which was run by C. E. Place and took his name. He was a grandfather of Mrs. Myrle McKim, widow of Ming McKim, foundry operator and mayor in the late 40's, now living in Baker. Spring Garden Avenue was bordered by Chinese vegetable gardens. Campbell was named for a Mr. Campbell who homesteaded on the river near the present street.

    I once asked how Resort Street got its name and was answered, "Why, from the resorts, of course."

    The original cemetery in Baker was on the hill now called Hillcrest. When this was moved several citizens secured the hill and surrounding land for development. Among them were Hardin Estes, R. D. Carter and Mike Wisdom. They plotted streets of which the names Carter and Estes remain. Wisdom Street is found only on very early maps.

    Much of the information in this article was obtained from "Oregon Geographic Names," by Lewis A. McArthur.

Pocahontas, the Town Named For an Indian Princess

The first roads in Baker County followed the foothills from Auburn to the north end of the valley. This served two priorities. First, the gold strikes were in the hills. Second, the valley floor was swampy and muddy. I. Hiatt says that the first country road established was from Auburn via Washington Ranch – or Washington Gulch – to Monhin's ranch on North Powder River.

There were several settlers at the north end who were developing farms. At least one, Arnst Loennig, traveled the road to Auburn to sell vegetables. Undoubtedly there were others. Some of the early settlers in that location were the A. H. Browns and the Poulsons.

John W. Wisdom, born March 15, 1840; died March 24, 1938. Wisdom and Dr. Boyd opened a drug store on the SW corner of Main and Valley streets at Baker City in 1867.

There were several little settlements in the hills but the one which has survived in our memory was Pine City, later known as Pocahontas. This was near the gold strikes on Salmon and Marble creeks. John Wisdom lived in this little community and made trips to The Dalles to bring in supplies. One trip took three months by wagon and ox team. He was gone from September to December. When he got home he found that his town had been moved down near the edge of the valley and had been renamed Pocahontas. There had always been a romantic interest in the Indian princess and this must have seemed a good name for their pretty little town. The location was near the present Ebell ranch where the road turns right toward Pine Creek and Rock Creek localities.

The people had been urged to make the change of location by John McLain and Wm. Hindman because they owned ranches on the edge of the valley and wanted to be on the road. This road was the main road to Haines and North Powder until well into the 1900's.

There was always a call to have a straight road through the valley and for some time the *Morning Democrat* put this slogan above its mast head: "A straight road to Haines." The road, when finally built, was really straight except for a couple of curves to accommodate the Chandlers and the Phillips.

Quite A town Developed

Pocahontas became quite an important little town. It had a hotel, an express office and a blacksmith shop. Also stores including one owned by Sam Baer who later moved to Baker and had a large department store for many years. His daughter, Elizabeth, thinks that Mr. Ottenheimer was associated with her father in Pocahontas.

The real fame of Pocahontas occurred when its citizens decided to get in the running for State Capital. Several towns in the Willamette Valley were rivals for the honor. One man had settled in Powder River Valley and was supporting the claim of Albany, his former residence. William Hindman entered the field with his home town, Pocahontas. The election was held in June, 1864, with the following results: Salem, 6,108 – Portland 3,854 – Eugene 1,588 and other places 577. Among the "others" Pocahontas received 10 votes.

Pocahontas remained quite a little community for a good many years although now there is nothing to be seen of it. The schoolhouse was the last to go. There are still people in Baker who attended the Pocahontas school.

The name Pocahontas remains to the present day to identify the road that led to the town. It is an

James School, District #3, established 1863, discontinued 1949. Located at intersection of Pocahontas and Wingville roads, 5 miles NW of Baker City.

important valley road and will gain more importance in years to come.

Every school child knows the story of Pocahontas in Virginia but not many people know about her later life.

She was converted to Christianity by the English colonists and married one of them, John Rolfe. He took her back to England where the little princess was welcomed by the English, always respectful of royalty.

But the Indian girl was homesick for her homeland. When finally she embarked at the London docks to go to Virginia it was too late. She died before the ship reached the sea. Her body was taken ashore at the town of Gravesend on the Thames. She was buried in St. George's Church. There is now a little park by the church with a statue of Pocahontas and a large billboard with the following inscription:

> ### ST. GEORGE'S CHURCH
> ### PRINCESS POCAHONTAS GARDENS
> *These gardens were opened and named Princess Pocahontas Gardens by His Worship the Mayor of Gravesend (Councilor L. W. Kempster, J. P.) on the occasion of a Gift of a Paten and Chalice to the Church by Her Majesty Queen Elizabeth II through the Lord —Bishop of Norwich on the 2nd, August 1958.*

His Excellency the American Ambassador was represented by His Personal Assistant, Mr. Ellis L. Phillips, Jr. who unveiled this record.

In the Chancel of this Church on March 21, 1617, was buried Princess Pocahontas, the first North American Christian, who had been received at the Court of King James I and who died on her return journey to Virginia.

The Church was destroyed by fire in 1727 and was rebuilt largely through the generosity and by the decree of George II. The Royal links have been extended and strengthened through this gracious gift of Her Majesty, who has recognized this hallowed spot as the first Christian tie with the American Nation.

Joaquin Miller, the Poet of The Sierras.

Joaquin Miller and the Canyon City Literary Society

Sometime in the eighteen-fifties Emeline McCallum and her father were riding from their grist mill at Oak Run in northern California to the town of Red Bluff. When almost there they were passed by a man riding very fast on a white horse. Thinking that he was carrying news they put their own horses to a gallop. When they came into town they found out that the news was that the man had stolen the horse and was now locked up in the log jail. The prisoner's name was Cincinnatus Heine Miller.

Several days later the news came to Oak Run that he had escaped. He had been living with the Digger Indians and his Indian wife had smuggled a saw to him. When the sheriff entered the jail he found that his guest had written poetry all over the walls.

Miller was quite young at this time and an admirer of Joaquin Murietta, the famous bandit. He adopted his nickname from him. This name, however, he used almost exclusively after becoming famous. Sometime after the horse-stealing incident the Indian wife was killed by settlers in a punitive expedition against the Indians.

In 1865 Emeline was living with her husband, G. I. Hazeltine, in Canyon City, Oregon. Who should turn up but C. H. Miller with his wife and baby. The present wife had been Minnie Myrtle Dyer of Southern Oregon. She was a poet in her own right and was the daughter of a well-known man in Port Orford. Mr. Packwood wrote in his memoirs that he had known Mr. Dyer and that he was a fine man.

Miller

Miller's character had improved since his time in California. He had sowed his wild oats and had returned to his family in Oregon. He became a respected citizen of Canyon City. He practiced law and was appointed County Judge by Governor Whitaker. In the same year he was a leader in a force to purse the Snake Indians. Lt. Waymire with a company of 25 soldiers came through Grant County from Harney County and was joined by C. H. Miller and a group of miners. The combined forces caught up with the Indians and defeated them.

The Millers had three children while living in Canyon City, one daughter, Maud, and two boys. Early in life, after leaving Canyon City, the boys seem to have disappeared and were erased from family records. Minnie Myrtle was considered by many people to be a better poet than her husband and some critics think that she influenced Joaquin's writings. They became more romantic than his earlier ones.

One of Miller's contributions to the community was the creation of a Literary Club. This was made up of men exclusively. The minutes of the club are left to us to read and are most interesting. The Secretary was T. C. Hyde, a cousin of the Hyde family in Baker. The members of the family in Baker included Charles F. Hyde, well known District Attorney, and Calvin Hyde.

The minutes are written in a beautiful, flowing hand, a penmanship we no longer see.

At the first meeting the members elected Judge Miller temporary Chairman and M. W. Fechheimer temporary Secretary. On a motion Miller, Fechheimer and Hyde were chosen for a committee to draft a constitution and bylaws for the government of the society. The meeting was adjourned to meet at the Courthouse on Friday evening, Dec. 21, 1866.

At the second meeting a constitution was adopted, also bylaws. The necessary officers were then elected: F. Adams, President; E. Lester, Vice President; T. C. Hyde, Secretary; A. G. Mulkey, Sergeant-at-arms; H. H. Hyde, Treasurer. The following persons were admitted as members: F. Adams, A. G. Nash, E. Lester, J. Abramson, G. Kohlberg and A. G. Mulkey.

The minutes continue:

"We the undersigned, do declare ourselves an Association for mental improvement, due consideration for the feelings of others, perfect command of temper in all our intercourse and seek for truth in all our exercises."

"Persons over 15 to be members."

"Honorary members any age."

The By Laws were, in part:

"Meet every Thursday evening."

"Meet annually on the Fourth of July to celebrate anniversary of our National independence." (On reading this we wonder if the members were present on the occasion when the speaker of the day read part of the Constitution of the U. S. before someone pulled his coattail and suggested he change to the Declaration of Independence.)

"Any person intending to propose a candidate for membership

shall submit his name and occupation to the club. He must get a two-thirds vote. Admittance fee $1.00. Dues 25 cents a month, payable in advance."

"No improper language."

"Fine 25 cents for two absences."

"Rules of debate:

"President shall state sides."

"No one shall speak more than once until everyone has spoken who wishes."

"President shall decide all debates on merits of arguments."

"At any meeting club may choose a member to deliver an essay, subject to be chosen by committee."

Names of members:

C. H. Miller – F. Adams – A. J. Nash – E. Lester – J. Abramson – M. W. Fechheimer – G. Kohlberg – A. J. Mulkey – T. C. Hyde – H. H. Hyde – J. W. Whalley – C. H. Wright – B. Whitten – J. W. Baldwin – D. C. Overhold – H. Kinzey – David Busley – J. Reynolds.

Subjects for debates:

"Resolved: That the doctrine of states rights as taught by Jefferson, Madison and Monroe is guaranteed to the respective states by the Constitution and is necessary to the maintenance of their equality.

"Resolved: That the sentiment in the following couplet is correct: of forms of government let fools contest what's best administered is best."

"Resolved: That elective franchise should be extended to every adult male inhabitant in the U. S. who can read and write and who does not give allegiance to a foreign power and to none others."

"Resolved: That discovery of gold on Pacific coast has been beneficial to mankind."

"Resolved: Should a uniform system of common school education be established and supported by our state government?"

"Resolved: Should the gold and silver mineral lands of the U. S.

be surveyed and sold by the general government?"

"Resolved: Should U. S. assume protectorate over Mexico?"

"Resolved: Should observance of Sabbath, commonly called Sunday, be enforced by statute?"

"Resolved: That mother exerts greater influence over character of child than father."

It is too bad that we will never know how these debates came out.

After Leaving Canyon City

Miller's stay in Canyon was not long and he began traveling in the U. S. and abroad, particularly in England where he was made much of. He had attained a reputation as a poet by this time. In England he always dressed in flannel shirt and knee high boots. He said that this was a costume the English expected of Americans. When in Canyon City he had often worn his trousers with one pants leg tucked in his boot and the other hanging loose. Some of his pictures show this. He was always a show off. He had adopted the nickname of Joaquin in California but did not use it much in Oregon. It became popular later.

After coming back to the U. S. he went into newspaper work in Washington D. C. as correspondent for numerous papers. He and Minni Myrtle had been divorced years before and in Washington he took a third wife, Miss Abby Leland. They had one child, Juanita.

He returned to California in 1887, to build a hill top home near Oakland. This became the Mecca for poets and admirers from many lands.

Lewis A. McArthur, writing in *The Oregonian*, April 22, 1937, told of a visit to Joaquin Miller:

"About twenty years ago when I was a student at the University of California I resolved to pay a call on Joaquin Miller, then living at his picturesque home in the hills east of Oakland. It was a long trip, on foot, on a warm day as I remember it. The great poet was still in bed though it was after noon and he was enveloped in a long yellow silk dressing gown. His fancy leather boots hung on the post at the foot of the bed and the bed itself was strewn with his writings.

"He told me many stories about Canyon City. When I was ready to leave he said, 'Well, my boy, I always owed your father a debt of gratitude. He did me a great service. We were both candidates for a Grant County convention. I was not happy about it at the time but later realized that he had done me a good turn and told him so. I would have been a failure as a county official but I have turned out to be a pretty fair poet. Since then I have thought that my thanks were due to Judge L. L. McArthur, who unintentionally made me change my career.'"

On A Later Visit

In 1907 Miller returned to Canyon City for a visit. Grandmother introduced me to him. He bent over and kissed me on top of the head and said, "Little girl, some day you will be proud to say that you have been kissed by Joaquin Miller." Sure enough, here I am telling about it.

Canyon City – Well known photographer, G. I. Hazeltine in foreground with the Grant County Courthouse above him. The courthouse was built in 1885. Lack of trees around the courthouse indicate it was just recently completed.

PART TWO
Gold or Jade?
The Chinese in the Mining Area

O.H. Fong and daughters, Marjorie and Christine.

When gold was discovered in California in 1849, the news reached China almost as soon as it was learned on the East Coast of the United States. Ships crossed the Pacific from California and sailed to the South coast of China, usually to the Canton district. For this reason the Chinese who came to California were all from the Canton area, particularly from the region of Toishan.

America became known to the Chinese as Gum Shan (the mountain of gold) and young men had a great desire to come to the fabulous country. They found several ways to reach their goal. Sometimes a collection was taken up in the community; sometimes funds came from neighbors and friends. Other youths became stowaways.

The first ones to arrive in San Francisco formed themselves into the Six Companies, so called from the six districts from which they came. Representatives from these companies met those arriving later at the docks and took charge of their compatriots. They found places for them to live and helped them to find work. By 1851 there were 25,000 Chinese in California.

There were people in the mining camps from countries all over the world, Britain, Germany, France, Australia and many other places, but the ones called foreigners by the miners were always the Chinese. There were several reasons for this feeling. The Celestials [Chinese] spoke little English, were independent, stayed to themselves, and were extremely hard workers. They provided real competition as they demanded little and were willing to work for less. Feeling rose against them and in every mining camp a law was included which prevented "Chinese and Tartars" from owning claims. They were allowed to work for wages.

If work in the mines was not available the Chinese turned to work in which they could be independent. Two occupations were laundries and restaurants. To open a laundry required only a little capital. Needed were a scrub board, soap, iron and board, and a place to heat the iron. (There was in Baker at one time a stove left from a Chinese laundry. It was round and there were hooks all around the stove on which to hang the irons.)

The Work Which They did

Laundries in busy San Francisco were greatly needed by the miners and other men, since there were few women in the city and most of them were not washer women. The men wore hard, detachable shirt fronts which cost $48 per dozen to wash and iron. Sometimes they were sent clear to Hawaii to be washed. Often it was 6 to 8 weeks before they came back. The Chinese laundries were a great boon.

A laundry needed little work space as the clothes would be collected and delivered. The Chinese had a custom of sprinkling which might have been objectionable to some but it was efficient. The laundryman filled his mouth with water and it came out in a fine spray to do the sprinkling. (An old Chinese wash house was still in Baker in recent times. It was located between the White Apartments and the home of the *Democrat-Herald*. This little building had been moved from the opposite corner to make room for the erection of the Antlers Hotel.)

Eating places provided another need. The Chinese were naturally good cooks and many of them were growing vegetables. The men of San Francisco liked their way of preparing food and their restaurants flourished. Two stories are told maybe true, maybe not, but they could be. One night several men came to a restaurant after it had run nearly out of food. They demanded a meal so the proprietor cut up everything that was left, added a little meat and some vegetables and mixed it with soy sauce, and thus "Chop Suey" was born. Another tale is that noodles were accidentally dropped into hot fat and when it was discovered how delicious they were, they became "Chow Mein."

They Worked Building the Railroad

When the great transcontinental railroad was being built from the East at one end and California from the other, competition between the two builders became very keen. Both were rushing to a junction in Utah. The Union Pacific had the Irish at work but there was no such labor force on the Pacific Coast to be hired by the Central Pacific.

Charles Crocker first thought of bringing peons from Mexico, but it could not be arranged. He now thought of the Chinese. Thousands of them were in California eking out a living by working old mining claims, growing vegetables and like work. Almost nobody believed that the Chinese, who averaged around 110 pounds, were strong enough to stand the Sierra climate and do the heavy work.

Crocker began by hiring fifty of them and took them to the end of the track. They quickly established a neat camp, cooked their rice and went to sleep. By sun up the Chinese were up too and at their picks and shovels. Twelve hours later Crocker sent for more Chinese. In six months there were two thousand Chinese hard at work. Some were brought directly from Canton. They continued to the end of the construction. Later they played a large part in the construction of the Canadian Pacific.

Chinese In The Mining Country

The working out of the California mines and Crocker's experience started the Chinese to head for the mines in the Inland Empire. Some went on their own but most were brought in by contractors often called boss men. For the newcomers from China at least, there was needed someone to translate for them and to make the working arrangements.

They traveled to the mining areas all over the Inland Empire. In Montana they were thought to number 800 in 1869, and in British Columbia in 1866 they numbered 1800 out of a total population of 13,800. In early days they were sometimes bought and sometimes kidnapped. When brought by contractors the contractors provided the outfit and transportation and required repayment.

For some reason the Indians hated the Chinese even more than they did the whites and often attacked the traveling companies. One time in the Owyhee Mountains the Snakes massacred a whole company.

Some independent men came to the camps to start laundries and eating places. The Chinese were treated fairly well in Idaho although a law passed, copied from California law, which taxed the "Mongolian" $5 a month. The reason for this was that the Chinese owned no property and could not be reached by ordinary taxation.

It could not be denied that the Chinese contributed a great deal toward the economy of the mining districts. By 1870 most of the mines were being worked by the Chinese, and they performed needed services in laundry work, growing vegetables, as cooks and other household servants and as woodchoppers. They were obedient, patient, imitative and quick to learn. They were peaceful and hard workers.

In the late sixties the gold mines had so deteriorated that most claims were turned over to them. The yield from their work was probably greater than was realized at the time. A good deal of money was sent back to China and they always took care of themselves. Sometimes they did extremely well. In 1958 an Idaho paper told of the death of a woman in Hong Kong. She had been born in Idaho City in 1888, the granddaughter of Loke Kee who made a fortune in gold.

The original First National Bank of Baker, now the U. S. National Bank, owns some records of the gold sent to the mint by the Chinese and others from Baker. There are a good many Chinamen listed.

As an example here is the amount sent to the mint by Lee Chung. Over a period of from 1890 through 1898, nine years, he sent in gold to the amount of $38,604.56 and silver to the amount of $261.71. This was an income not to be sneezed at even now, a large sum for that time.

Some others listed as sending in gold and receiving payment were Long Bur, Lee Chang, Hong Chung, Ah Jim, Hong Lee, Took Kee, Ah Dic, Sam Lung, King Sing, Fi Chong, Quing Wing Chung, He Pong, Chin Lee and So Jo. All of them sent in varying amounts adding up to a lot of gold.

The Chinese At Sparta

William H. Packwood has left an account of his experiences with the Chinese workers. He said, in part:

"I was planning a ditch to bring water to the mines out in the Eagle Mountains. People tried to discourage me, one man saying, 'Packwood, I don't believe that water and mines should ever come together.'

"I worked all Fall with a Civil Engineer, Charles Foster, and with Alex Stewart and Charley Awah until the snow became so deep at times, we were compelled to shovel off snow at night to get a place to pile brush, on which we rolled up our blankets at night and kept a log fire going to keep warm by. The Chinaman packed and moved camp for us. From what I learned I determined to build the ditch....

"After making arrangements for money, etc., I hired Charley as interpreter to write letters to different China companies telling them I was going to build a ditch to the old Kooster mines and would give contracts. I was to pay Charley $900 for a year. This was about February 1871....

"A ten-stamp mill was purchased from the Gem mine. Whites had come in rapidly and located the mining claims. Chinamen came in to get contracts and secure claims.

"The first contract I let was to Ah Fat, a China company that had worked for me on the Eldorado ditch. It was for the first 1 and 2 miles. I made out a blank form of contract, stating all particulars as to payment, etc., leaving only to be filled in, the details as to the ground contracted. I had studied the situation and made up my mind, first, that $26,000.00 was nothing like the amount of money the ditch would cost; I did not propose to bear all the risks. The Chinamen would be very much benefited and should bear part of the risks. I put in the contract: That on each contract after deducting cash paid and supplies furnished the balance would be due and payable in three and six months time after I ran water to Rattlesnake Gulch, the first mining ground, on 1st and 2nd mile, Ah Fat's contract, about six miles from Sparta.

"There was a man at Sparta with a small store, Capt. I. H. Fisk. One of the contractors on 16th mile, Le Taw, showed Fisk his contract. Fisk saw the Rattlesnake clause, 3 and 6 months time. He told Le Taw that I could not complete the ditch and unless I ran water to Rattlesnake nothing would come due them, that I could stop the work, in fact gave Le Taw quite a scare. Le Taw saw the other contracts all the same.... A runner was sent up to the head of the ditch for me to be certain to come down Sunday to 12th mile camp where all the chiefs would be for supplies.

"I got down to 12th mile camp on Sunday. We called all the Chinamen and had them sit in a circle same as done by Indians in an early day when treaties were made. There was Le Taw and I and Awah, the interpreter. Le Taw said what Fisk said about it and then they wanted to know what I said about it. I said Fisk told the truth about the contract but he was not truthful when he said I would hold up finishing the ditch to withhold payment. I said they had been paid so far. They agreed. I told them I proposed having them share in the loss if there was any and if the ditch was finished they would all be gainers and my purpose was to finish the ditch as soon as possible. 'Now,' I said. 'Put on every man you can get, work long hours and in three and six months after I run water there you will all be paid.' I gave them a clear cut talk. They all went away and considered what they would do.

"After some time they all came back and as soon as the meeting was in order their spokesman got up and said, 'Now, Mr. Packwood, if the China companies heap hurry, dig him ditch will you heap hurry flumes and tunnel and rock so water can run through ditch this year?' I told them I would put on extra men and do my very best for them to put on all the men they could and I would run the water through as soon as done. They said 'Alright, Mr. Packwood, China Company will hurry work on ditch.' That was the turning point. I never saw work progress faster. Our balances were paid 3 and 6 months from October 14, 1871, and thoroughly satisfactory.

Credit to The China Josh

"Some said I built the ditch but I claim the credit is due to the China Josh of Ah Fat Co. One day I said to Ah Sing, my rodman, 'What's the matter with these Chinamen, they must think I have plenty of money, but I have not and they may lose by working for me.'

"He says, 'Mr. Packwood, you no savvy, Chinamen heap savvy.' This was to me a queer proposition, that the Chinamen should know more about my ability to pay them than I did myself. So I insisted on Sing's telling me what the Chinamen savvied that I did not. He then said what it was they savvied.

"He said that at the time my letters were sent out to China companies one of the letters was at Ah Fat's company's camp on Rock Creek west of Baker, that the Chinamen were having a big Free Mason time, many of them being Masons.

(The Chinese had been Masons in San Francisco, having their own lodges, never integrating with the whites. They have their lodges to this day. Incidentally, the Blacks also have their own Masonic lodges.)

Chinese Joss which was located in the Chinese Temple in Baker City.

Sources for history of the Chinese in the mining area:
   Holbrook, Stewart, *Story of American Railroads*
   Sung, Betty Lee, *Mountain of Gold*
   Timble, W. J., *Mining Advance into the Inland Empire*
   Packwood, W. H., *Handwritten Memoirs*.
   Records of Gold Sent to the Mint, By Permission of the United States National Bank of Baker.

Chinese symbol for gold

Ki Ki, who was manager of On On Co., a general store located across the alley from the Neuberger-Heilner store.

"Sing said my letters were being considered and it was proposed to consult Ah Fat's Josh as to what to do. He says, 'You long time savvy Ah Fat's Josh on Eldorado ditch.' I told him I did very much. It was a small wooden Josh about 12 to 15 inches high, placed on the bank of the ditch with a light always kept burning before it. And now it was on the Sparta ditch on 1st and 2nd mile contract at Ah Fat's camp. I often stopped to look at it.

"Sing said that the China priest was called and he had strips of paper on which they wished answers from the Josh. The old priest went through certain performances, talked and set fire to the slips of paper and from the way they fell the priest decided the answer. In this case the question was to know whether to go to work for me. The Josh said, 'Packwood velly good man, Chinamen work Packwood, catchee money all right.'

"Sing said that this Josh was over two hundred years old, belonged to the Ah Fat family and never fooled Chinamen. So, now I know why Ah Fat company led off for 2 mile contract and why this Chinaman believed I would be all right as pay.

"We built the ditch for over $90,000.00 with Josh's endorsement."

Mr. Packwood said at a later time that while the ditch was being built there were about 500 white men and 1,000 Chinese living in Sparta. He said, "You could smell the opium a mile away." This was one of the comforts in their hard working lives, living as they did so far from home with no families. There were very few Chinese women ever in America until much later times. Another pleasure was gambling.

Other settlers in the Sparta neighborhood told of the Chinese and many of them swore by the Chinese doctor. Mable Binns, a postmaster there in later years and a historian, wrote that the last Chinese in Sparta was Ah Wing. He later died in Baker. She said that he delighted the children by playing his banjo and singing "Yankee Doodle."

1870 And Thereafter

The Chinese mined for many years after the white people had given up many of the mines as worked out. James. L. Kraft, late President of the Kraft Cheese Company, once wrote a book on his hobby. It is called *Adventures in Jade*, unfortunately now out of print. It was Mr. Kraft's opinion that the Chinese were looking for jade as well as gold. And perhaps they found some, especially in Northern California. There is some jade in Baker County, rather dark in color and of not very high quality.

"The Chinese had an interest in jade for religious reasons. It has been associated with religious usage from the dawn of civilization. From the earliest days in China jade pieces of varying colors represented heaven, earth and the four quarters. To civilized men from the beginning of time, Jade, the sacred stone of the Orient, has symbolized truth, goodness and purity – man's mystic relationship to his Creator and his pledge of good will toward his fellow man." — from "Light in the Window," published by Kraft Cheese Company.

The Exclusion Laws

In California by 1870 gold was getting more difficult to find and the hard-working Chinese were getting more than the whites of what there was.

The Orientals were content with less and would work for lower wages. The frustrations of the Californians were taken out on the Chinese. And they were strange. Politicians began to take up the question, as they often did and still do now, they made a larger issue of it than it deserved. They said, "The Chinese must go." Soon people were aroused and sometimes Chinese were stoned, robbed and murdered. Prejudice followed them everywhere. It seems not to have been so bad in Oregon as elsewhere.

The issue was taken to Congress. Representatives of other States were not especially interested, but, in the manner that politics works, the Californians gained support in return for favors to the other fellow.

In 1881 Congress passed a bill to suspend Chinese immigration for 20 years. President Arthur vetoed it. Another bill suspended immigration for 10 years. This was the infamous Chinese Act of 1882. This bill applied only to laborers, but everyone was called a laborer, even physicians or professors. This was a very great hardship for many of these people, as they took the long, expensive trip to America, only to be turned back on arrival.

One of its tragic results was to prevent wives and families from joining their men. Most of the men had to live without a woman in their lives as there was no one for them to marry. Only a few women and also some sons were allowed to enter.

Between 1882 and 1924, 14 pieces of legislation against the Chinese were passed. There was the Scott Act and the Geary Act which practically stripped Chinese of any protection in the Courts. In 1892 the Exclusion Acts were renewed for 10 years.

When Franklin Roosevelt became President he said, "We must acknowledge our mistakes." Public sentiment was for repeal, and the Chinese were our allies in the Second World War. The bill for repeal was passed on October 22, 1943.

There was a couple in Baker who were victims of these vicious laws. An Englishman named Tom Smith moved to the John Day Valley and bought a ranch. He brought with him a large family and a retinue of English servants. At the same time there was a famous Chinese cook at Austin Stage Station, in the location of the present Bates. This cook, Poe, married one of the English maidservants and she accompanied him to China. Years later I met her in Baker and she told me of her life in China. She said, "I was happy in China. The family treated me so well. But, my husband was not allowed to leave China and I was not allowed to stay." Mrs. Poe died several years later in St. Elizabeth Hospital, Baker City.

After The Gold Rush

Many Chinese left Baker after the first gold rush was over, but a good many stayed and became part of the community. They built a Chinatown at the location of Resort and Auburn and running back to the river. This was before there was a bridge on Auburn. In 1883 they built a fine Joss House costing $10,000.00. It was one of the few good buildings built by the Chinese. Loy Wisdom remembers visiting the Joss House on each Chinese New Year's day. The lower floor was filled with bunks holding Chinamen smoking opium with long pipes. Upstairs was the religious part of the building which held the Joss. The opium was sent to them by mail in tobacco tins.

Bill Patterson says that he was once sent by his mother to find a man named "An Gow" to work for her. He first went to the Wing Hing Yuen Company to inquire. This was a good sized store extending along Resort which sold products used by the Chinese. Bill was sent to the rear of the store where the lots had been filled with the little cubicles, each surrounded by a high board fence. Each had a gate in front and another one out the back connecting with the next little shack. He went in and out until he finally found the man he was hunting. We have some checks made out to An Gow endorsed on the back with his character.

The Chinese ran laundries and eating places and grew vegetables. Some of the gardens were on Spring Garden Avenue and some on the west side of town toward the foothills. The truck they produced was always earlier than from other gardens. The men peddled the vegetables in the traditional fashion from two baskets hanging from a yoke across their shoulders. Housewives sometimes went to the gardens to choose their vegetables.

There was a woman in Baker City who trained Chinamen to be cooks, one at a time. When each became proficient she found him a job in a home and began to train the next one. Consequently, several Baker City homes had fine cooks. They became martinets of the kitchen. The housewife entered her own kitchen with fear and trembling. They chased the kids but this was great fun for all, no hard feelings.

I remember with affection my father's friend, Ah Ben, in Burns and old How, who worked for Dr. Ashford in Canyon City, and others. Every China New Years we looked forward to the gifts they brought; China candy, Chinese nuts (lichee nuts) and embroidered silk handkerchiefs. The Chinese always settled all accounts at the New Year.

The Chinese graveyard was on a hill east of town. Where we put flowers on graves, the Chinese put food and other things for use in after life. Little boys loved to steal the food. This was disrespectful and no joke. As far as stealing goes, a good many flowers disappear now on Memorial Day and are probably not stolen by children.

The Baker Health Department kept records of all deaths and, when enough time had passed for the remains to be skeletons, the Chinese dug them up and returned the bones to the homeland sending them out through the port of Seattle. Courtney Gray worked in 1910 and 1920 for Dr. Huff who was the health officer at that time. She said that very careful records were made of names, dates of death, etc. There is only one grave in the old cemetery now and it dates only from the nineteen thirties.

There are old tales of the way the Chinese were treated in the early days. There were some bad incidents of robbery and murder, but there seems to have been little of the mindless cruelty that occurred in other areas, such as riders lassoing Chinese on foot.

Little boys loved to wait on the sidewalk and pull the pigtails as the men passed. Not too serious and perhaps a natural thing for a little boy to do. The queue or pigtail was not the choice of the Chinese men themselves. It was a symbol of subjugation forced upon them by the ruling Manchus. In 1911 when the Manchus were overthrown, the Chinese could cut off the queues, and most of them did.

Several years ago an old store was opened in John Day. This was the Kam Wah Chung Company. It was closed up after the death of Dr. Ing Hay, who had practiced medicine in Grant County for a long time. For some reason it was opened and investigated, and there were found many things left over from the Chinese past. These included bottles of medicine, old whiskey, etc., but the most interesting thing was a pile of letters perhaps received from China. A young scholar attending Portland State University from Taiwan began the translation. Whether this has continued is not known. This scholar, of course, could not go to the mainland for any help. If these letters can be deciphered, it should shed some light on history and be of great help to students of the times.

Ah Fong was one of the last known Chinese people of this era to leave McEwen, photo taken in 1910.

PART THREE
The Second Gold Rush: 1890 – 1914
Days of Elegance

O.H.P. McCord and Charles Ernst in 1897. Winners of the Cake Walk at a dance given by the Degree of Honor Lodge, Baker City.

Edith Ganzaga Packwood Rand (1871-1954), wife of John Langdon Rand and mother of author, Helen Biggs Rand. This is Edith's 1888 graduation photo. She was in the first class to graduate from St. Francis Academy in Baker City.

This is a corner of the living room of the house on the Young Ranch, Sumpter Valley, Oregon.

Main Street at Court from a 1907 Postmarked Card, Baker City.

Washington St. looking west from Geiser Grand Hotel on Main Street, Baker City

Not long ago I remarked to a group of Baker women that their town in the nineties and early nineteen hundreds had been a place of great elegance. I was answered by cries of "Baker elegant? You are kidding." However, that period was a time of elegance everywhere. It had begun in the eighteen eighties, continued through the nineties and reached its peak during the reign of Edward the Seventh in England. It ended at the beginning of the First World War.

Baker City at the time was in the middle of the second gold rush. It had busy lumber mills and was the terminus for the Sumpter Valley railroad. This gold rush was not so much concerned with prospecting as in earlier years, although some prospecting went on all the time and continues to this day. At the center of the action were properties already discovered and that were being financed by Eastern money. Sumpter and Bourne were at the center of this activity and were bustling towns. The metropolis of Baker City was full of outside businessmen, promoters and investors. A great deal of money was being circulated and local residents prospered.

A busy social life was in full swing, centered in homes, the Geiser Grand Hotel, the Elks Club and the Baker Opera House. Also, about 1915 a country club was built at the east end of Washington Avenue. It was promoted by Ray Nye of Nebraska, a stockholder in the Eastern Oregon Power and Light Company. This club building is the one that was occupied by the Fireside Restaurant. It commanded a beautiful view over the town and the Elkhorn Mountains. There were golf links on the flat below the club. The open air swimming pool was nearby, using water from Sam-O hot springs. These springs were named for Sam Ottenheimer, who promoted them. These springs also provided sparkling water for the bottling works which produced Sam-O-soda pop.

Many parties and dances took place at the club. But, the really elegant dances were given in the beautiful Elks' Club which served the lodge and community till it was razed to construct the present building. The Elks sponsored a New Year's Ball every year and this Ball was the height of the social season. Those of us too young to attend were taken to watch for a time from the balcony. The women's gowns often came from the famous dressmakers, the Shogrens, in Portland. The gowns usually had trains and they had a loop which the lady held in her hand to keep the train off the floor while she danced. Her coiffure was elaborate and helped by false hair called switches. One lady lost hers while dancing, picked it up and waved it in the air while she danced on. The dances were usually waltzes, two-steps and an occasional polka or schottische. The gentlemen, some of them, wore formal evening dress, white tie and tails, not dinner coats as they do today. The Ball was always opened with a grand march, beautifully performed.

Homes, Center of Social Life

The homes, however, were the center of social life. There were dinners, teas and card parties. Domestic help was available and several homes employed Chinese cooks. The Baker women were fabulous cooks and trained their help well.

The teas always provided entertainment, music of some kind. This era was before radio and television, but there was fine local talent. Often there would be one or two large card parties in one week, several women entertaining together. Many obligations could be paid back at once. Social card playing progressed over the years from whist to five hundred, auction bridge and finally contract. Special tables were included for those who had not learned the latest version. Luncheon was usually served. I once helped with a party that was given in a home for three successive days with a three course luncheon and ten tables of cards each day.

Calling Was More Formal

Paying calls continued at all times. There were strict rules. A call never lasted longer than fifteen minutes. Calling cards were left even if no one was at home. I often came home from school to find cards under the door which I carefully placed in the card tray in the entrance hall. The husband's card was left for both wife and husband but a lady's card was never left for the man of the house.

Several calls would be made in one day and Bob Bettner's cab would be hired. Many people owned horses but not all had barns. The horses were kept in livery stables and it was sometimes a nuisance to get them out. Some ladies had an "At Home" day. This day was printed in the bottom corner of the card and the hostess stayed home that day and served tea.

The men of the town had their own games but they could hardly be called elegant. The game was poker and some of the legends of the games are still around. One or two well-known men of the times lost more than their shirts. They lost all they had made in the mines.

Another adult male occupation was frequenting the saloons. All were on the east side of Main Street. As young girls we were told to stay on the west side of the street. This was all right with us as the fine stores were on that side, Neuberger & Heilner, Weil's and Baer's clothing stores. And then there were the really important places, Baker's Bakery and later Glenn Miller's ice cream parlor. There we had a phosphate for five cents or if in the money a ten-cent sundae. We had little money because, although we did a great deal of babysitting, we never received pay for it.

One place downtown on the east side of the street was Baker's first Nickelodeon which we could attend on Saturday afternoon but never on Sunday. We watched Mary Pickford and her contemporaries but didn't know their names as names of actors were considered unimportant in the early movies. There was always a magic lantern show of slides accompanied by a song to go with the picture. The colors on the slides were always a little off center.

On one social occasion the men's and women's amusements coincided with hilarious results. The wife was entertaining with a large party. When she was upstairs changing into her party finery her husband came in and the full punch bowl tempted him to mischief. He added a little flavor in the form of a bottle of whiskey. It was a lively party. Only a few ladies were familiar with the taste of bourbon but thought the punch the best they had ever tasted. The few who knew what they were drinking thoroughly enjoyed the spectacle of the innocents. It was the talk of the town. The husband's marriage was in grave danger for some time.

Masonic and Eastern Star picnic near Sumpter; wagons were for transportation to the country.

Band Shell in Geiser-Pollman Park in Baker on Mother's Day, May 12, 1929.

Summertime Activities

In the summer formality was largely forgotten. Life in Baker County in the warm weather was as delightful as it is now. First there was the swimming pool at Sam-O Springs, outdoors, which was reached by buggy, surrey with the fringe on top, bicycle, model T or just on foot.

There was professional baseball, some years in a Tri-State league with Idaho and Washington. The ball park was out on Valley Avenue. All games were played in the daytime and it was a thrill to hear the crack of the ball on a hot summer afternoon. On Wednesday evenings there was a concert by the Baker Band which, at different times was called by different names. For a long time it was the White Swan Band. It was conducted by Louis Freitag. [Louis Freitag's daytime job was as a jeweler.] These concerts were held on Main Street until the band shell was built in the park. The annual summer carnival was also held on Main Street.

Picnics happened all summer long at Ebell Park, Marble, Pine and other creeks. They started early in the day as it took longer to go and come. Eagle Creek was too far for a one-day excursion. That was the country for a camp of a week or more. Fish were plentiful without stocking as were grouse and sage hen, practically gone now. And huckleberries!

One vehicle used for picnics was a tally-ho owned by Bob Bettner and his pride and joy. It took lively groups on picnics and excursions. It was a high, open coach pulled by four horses, a holdover from the British fox hunt. It was a great sight to watch it come down the street with passengers blowing horns and crying "Tally-ho!"

Baker Residents Travelled

Baker people were always great travelers. After all, the country was settled by travelers. People went all over the U.S. by way of the comfortable passenger trains and some abroad by ship. Colonel and Mrs. Ayres and her mother went everywhere in the world that people could conveniently go and-inconveniently, too.

Arthur Swift, Baker High School Class of 1893.

The most famous traveler in the county was Arthur Swift, who lived on a farm with a big, red barn out on Pocahontas road. Mr. Swift had been a commercial traveler and had gone by the way of horse and buggy into every county in the U.S. He could name all the counties and county seats in the U.S. by request. He made Ripley's "Believe It or Not." He was a member of the Oregon legislature at one time.

The trips of most people were made to Portland. Even for a few days trip, a lady would take a trunk which was picked up by Charley Emerson's express-wagon—later Bill Ellis'—and taken to the depot. One lady recalled that they always stayed at the old Portland Hotel, now torn down. She said that unless they were going to the theater the whole evening's entertainment would consist of dinner at the hotel. Red carpets would be laid in the lobby to protect the ladies' trains. There was music and a long, leisurely dinner.

Baker residents, if they went at no other time, went to Portland for the Rose Festival in June. Travel in Portland at that time was by trolley. One of the events of the festival was the night parade with electric-lighted trolleys. Alas, all this will never come again.

First Street, looking south from Center (Broadway) Street. Packwood house and Parker's Studio in foreground. Antlers Hotel is at left, when just two stories tall.

Some Old Houses ...and the People Who Lived in Them

There are six old houses well known to the people of Baker. There are others not usually recognized at this time.

The dwellings most familiar are the Wisdom house, the Ison house, the Heilner home and the three built from the same plan and paid for with the gold from the Baisley-Elkhorn mines. These three are presently occupied by Leo Adler, the Walter Gildersleeves and Mrs. Clara Adams.

The home of Loy Wisdom at 2035 2nd and Broadway is unique in many ways. It has the first large house built in the little community. The date was 1878. It has been continuously occupied by the same family. Loy, who lives there now, is the daughter of John Wisdom who had it constructed. It has the original furnishings bought in San Francisco, even the window hangings. The house and furniture are beautiful and have been so well kept over the years. Perhaps one could say that the Wisdom house is Baker's outstanding structure from the past.

Two of the Baisley houses are on Main Street between Baker and Madison streets. The Adler home had several owners before being purchased by Carl Adler. The Gildersleeve home was built for Sam Baer, who lived there with his family until his death. It has the same plan as the Adler house except that it is reversed.

The home of the Baisleys themselves is on the old farm on Pocahontas Road. It had been preceded by a log cabin built by Sam Baisley. The present house is occupied by Mrs. Clara Adams, whose husband was a nephew of Sam. It was probably built in the middle eighties and keeps some of its original look including original wall paper. Sam Baisley always had one of the best gardens in the area. He brought produce into the town. Pickle-making always waited on Mr. Baisley's cucumbers.

The Ison house is on the corner of Washington and Resort streets. It was owned by Judge Luther B. Ison and lived in by the family until the death of Mrs. Ison. Their children were Dr. Virgil Ison and Mrs. Alex (Edna) MacDougall. There was another daughter who died young. When Virgil married he lived next door but the MacDougalls lived with Mrs. Ison until her death, afterwards moving to Portland. The house is presently being repaired and redecorated. It has fine interior woodwork.

The Heilner home was built and occupied by one of Baker's earliest citizens, Sigismund Heilner, who married Miss Clara Neuberger of Portland. Their son, Joe Heilner, remembered that the house was built in 1887. Mr. Heilner's life deserves a whole article. He was born in Bavaria and came to America in 1853. In 1865 he took merchandise to the Inland Empire, sold it and also taught painting to the miners, a talent he had pursued in Germany. He returned to Portland, and after marrying, came to Baker County. He had his business for some time in Sparta (arriving there in 1872), building a stone store which is still standing. He moved to Baker City in 1874 and built a one-story store that later became the Neuberger & Heilner store. He expanded it to include three stories and a cupola around 1889.

The Heilner house is beautifully-kept by its present owner, Herman David, who was a nephew of Clara Neuberger Heilner.

Homes East of River

A beautiful old home is the one standing at 1614 Washington Street. It was built for Mr. and Mrs. Edmund Perkins, 1862 pioneers, and was the second house built on that side of the river. Some of Mr. Perkins' descendents live in Baker at this time. After settling in Baker City, Mr. Perkins returned to his home state of Missouri, driving an ox team. He came back to Baker in 1866 driving a fine team of Missouri mules.

Another home in the same neighborhood is the Moulton home at 1522 Washington Street. Mr. George Moulton came from Maine and engaged in mining in the West but did not come to Baker until 1885. He was always prominent in civic affairs being on the school board and a councilman. His daughter, Ella, was a well known citizen of the town, a leading educator.

George Moulton

The Sam Baer House

The Bishop House

The Mann House

The Dodson House

The Ison House

The Wisdom House

The Surbeck House

The Johns House

Several of the interesting homes of the early era have vanished. Dr. Atwood's home took up a whole block bounded by Main, Resort, Baker and Madison streets. It was torn down many years ago.

Mr. Faull had a very large house on Fourth Street. The Faull's elegant parties were the talk of Baker City. Later on, the son, Dr. Carleton Faull, made the house into a hospital, but after being used for several years, it burned down.

Dodson House

The home of Dr. O. M. Dodson was taken down only a few years ago. It stood on Resort Street facing down Court Street. It was built on the plan of an English house with the living rooms on the upper story and dining room and kitchen on the lower level. The front steps ascended from the ground to the upper story and there was an outside entrance on the lower level. The busy doctor had his telephone on the stair landing to serve both floors but that meant running up and down for every call, many in the middle of the night. The outside steps were usually graced by at least four hound dogs. They accompanied the doctor on every call. It was easy to spot the doctor's whereabouts.

Dr. O. M. Dodson leading a Baker City parade on horseback, accompanied by one of his hounds.

An old brick house, now lived in by Mrs. Fred Witham, stands at 1403 Broadway. It must have been built before 1900 as Mrs. Maude Witham remembers it as a child when attending Brooklyn school. It is a charming small house, having been improved by the Witham family.

The W. F. Butcher house stands at 1415 Dewey Avenue. It has been converted into an apartment house. The owner, Philip R. Bishop was an Englishman who came to Baker in 1865 and prospered in mining. Mr. Butcher bought it and lived there with a large family of children. Mr. Butcher was one of Baker's leading lawyers.

The house now occupied by Gray's Pioneer Chapel was built for Charles A. Johns and family who came to Baker in 1888. Mr. Johns practiced law with the firm of Hyde, Johns and Olmsted. The other partners were Charles F. Hyde, husband of Molly Packwood, first white child born in Auburn, and M. L. Olmsted, retired from the position of Judge of the Sixth Judicial District.

Notable Houses and Some Famous People

Mr. Johns was ambitious politically; and it was said that the cupola on the front porch of his house was installed as a place from which to accept the Governorship of Oregon. He never became Governor but he became an Associate Justice of the Oregon Supreme Court and in 1921 he was appointed Chief Justice of the Philippines, a position he held until his death.

The Johns house, with its large grounds at that time the scene of a notable party. It was a Japanese party, Japan having just come into world news at the time. The trees were decorated with Japanese lanterns and the guests all wore Japanese costumes.

The old home of George and Nea Small stands on the corner of Washington and Seventh streets. It has been made into apartments. Mr. Small and I. B. Bowen were the editors of the *Morning Democrat*. The Small house had both downstairs and upstairs living rooms and a small elegant parlor. The parlor had a white marble fireplace and was furnished with fragile gilt chairs, often looked at askance by visiting gentlemen. A conversation chair stood at one side made in the form of an "S" where two people could face each other as they chatted. Mrs. Small had a north studio upstairs where she painted and taught china painting. Some of her pieces are still around and anyone who has one owns a treasure. They are usually signed. She was the daughter of M. M. Hazeltine, Baker photographer, who was known all over the West.

The home of I. B. Bowen is on East Washington just beyond the river. It is painted a soft grey blue and is a large and comfortable house.

Across the street from the Bowen house was the house of the Moomaws. It is still standing. The son, Lewis Moomaw, became a famous Hollywood motion picture director. He produced a silent picture in Alaska, called *The Cheechakos*, pronounced Cheechawkers and meaning greenhorns in the Eskimo language. Lewis was accompanied to Alaska by Victoria Wellman, Baker's fine dressmaker, who designed costumes for the actors. It was a gala occasion when the movie was shown in Baker.

Another house was the John Dooley house at Broadway and Grove streets.

It was amusing to know that the John Laidys and the Peter Manns both lived on West Washington Street. The Laidy house was near the depot. The Mann house, an old stone house, is on the corner of Washington and Fourth just north of the Courthouse. It is presently being restored. Victoria Wellman roomed there until she moved to Portland and carried on her business from the top floor of the old Portland Hotel until it was torn down.

Lovely Homes Surviving the Decades

One of the loveliest homes in Baker is seldom seen nowadays due to the illness of its owners, the G. P. Lilleys. It is noted for its beautiful interior woodwork. It was built for Mr. and Mrs. Kadish who came to Baker in the nineties. When they left Baker it was sold to the William Pollmans, parents of Mrs. Lilley.

The old Geiser home is on Second and Madison and is owned by Mr. and Mrs. John Nash. Mrs. Nash is the granddaughter of the Geisers. They built the home in 1883, at that time "way out in the country." It is beautifully preserved by its owners.

When Mrs. Geiser came from Germany at the age of eighteen to join her sisters she met some people on the ship who borrowed money from her. From there they took her to Colorado. In Colorado she met and married John Geiser who was from Switzerland. Two of their children, Albert and Louisa, were born in Colorado. The family moved to San Francisco then to Oregon and finally to Baker where they stayed. Mrs. Geiser never joined her sisters.

Mr. Geiser invested in land and in 1891 bought the Bonanza mine from Mr. Ladd of Ladd and Tilton Bank. It was always a good gold producing mine, managed by the family. Miss Louisa was a good business woman and was involved in the mine management as she was later in the management of the Geiser Grand Hotel.

There is one interesting old home which no one seems to know about. It is an empty house at the end of Elizabeth Street. It could have dropped in right out of Germany. We think that the Surbeck brothers lived there at one time but do not know if they built it. Some old timers refer to the house as the cigar factory. The Surbecks did have a cigar factory on Court between Main and First. They also had a candy store and soda fountain. We had milk shakes there after the games.

Some Builders of Pioneer Homes

We must remember some builders. John Virginius Benes came to Baker to work in the mines but he turned to architecture and built some of Baker's finest homes. Mr. Benes was born in the country which is now known as Czechoslovakia and ran away from home at the age of fourteen with a circus and came to America. He was a cousin of Eduard Benes who was President of Czechoslovakia in 1935, resigned when the Germans occupied the Sudetenland, and who came to America, returning to his homeland in 1945 and was again elected President.

John Benes, after following mining for a time, turned to architecture and built some of Baker's finest homes, including the Lilley and Johns houses; and he also built the Sanitarium at Hot Lake. He drew the designs for the St. Francis Cathedral but left Baker to live in Portland leaving the construction to Tom Grant and Mike White.

Tom Grant was the builder of many of Baker's outstanding stone buildings. Besides the Cathedral he built the Priest's house, the Rand building and others. These buildings of native stone are unique to Baker and should be preserved for posterity. The stone came from the Pleasant Valley region.

St. Francis Cathedral. Built between 1905-1907, dedicated in spring of 1908.

The Gold City on the Opera Circuit

Late in the eighteen nineties the Heilig Theater Company of Portland and George L. Baker decided that they must have a stopover for the theatrical companies traveling from Salt Lake City to Portland. Baker was selected for several reasons. It was a good location and it was a prosperous town. Boise was considered but turned down because it was in Idaho and because it was off the main line of the railroad. Perhaps Mr. Baker liked the name of the Eastern Oregon town.

Baker business men were consulted and several consented to buy stock in the enterprise. The Heilner family led in this venture.

The Opera House opened in 1900, a large and imposing brick building. It was on the N.E. corner of Main and Church streets. There was a roomy lobby, a commodious main floor and four boxes, an upper and a lower, on each side of the stage. The stage was large and faced an orchestra pit. There was a lower balcony and this made something of a problem on the main floor as the supporting pillars interfered with a good view from a few of the back seat locations. The second balcony was reached by a steep stair and the seats were not reserved. This writer remembers climbing to the top and when faced with the precipitous descent from the landing at the top of the aisles to the seats, retreated in terror and never went back. This opera house was built in metropolitan proportions.

The stage had a permanent curtain with a scenic view in the center surrounded by advertisements of Baker City firms. This kept us entertained until the show started. Another entertainment was a metal box on the back of each seat. By inserting 25-cents, a box of chocolates appeared, pretty good size, too, for a quarter!

The Dedication of the Opera House

On the opening night the theater was filled to see the famous actor Frederick Ward in "The Court Jester." The box seats were occupied by the stockholders. John L. Rand [father of the author] made the opening address of which a copy remains to us:

"Ladies and Gentlemen: At the threshold of a new century we meet to dedicate this building to the high purpose for which it was destined. It reflects great credit upon, and will be of calculable benefit to the community. It is impossible for the tongue to frame fitting language to express the great debt of gratitude we owe to these far-seeing and public spirited men, who by their energy and money have presented this noble monument to Baker City for the education and entertainment of the public. Tonight we feel proud of our city, our people and of this magnificent structure and we sincerely thank those who have made this occasion possible. But it is not for this building alone that we are grateful—we thank them for causing to be present tonight, Mr. Ward, the greatest living representative of that noble profession which has made the names of Booth and Barrett immortal, and whom I now have the honor of presenting to you."

This play was only the first of the treasury of plays and music which the opera house provided for over thirty years. It seems likely that no other town of its size in the United States at that time had such good entertainment. Remember, these were not the usual traveling companies that visited small towns. It was big city fare, the top attractions of the country. Music included grand opera, sometimes for several nights in succession, and there were such concerts as that given by Madame Schumann-Heink, the Walter Damrosch Orchestra, Harry Lauder and Sousa's band. There was the fine drama of the time with top stars and the delightful light operas and musical comedies of the era.

The culture it provided worked both ways. Baker City already had a population which appreciated good theater and it acquired more education from the theatre itself.

Sanford Heilner has many recollections of the early days. He was a boy of sixteen at the opening. He was the first usher of which there were usually four on the main floor and two on the first balcony. One of the first things that he noticed was that, although there were fire escapes, they had no inside light to inform people of the location. With his own money he bought the red lights and had them installed. Mr. Baker praised him for his thoughtfulness.

Later, Sanford had a large part in the running of the theater. He sold tickets at the box office but they were also sold at Levinger's Drug

Store which had opened in 1898. Over a time Sanford was given more responsibility and dealt with the manager who traveled with the company. They settled their money transactions after the first act. Sometimes the company had to take a train immediately after the performance.

The Founder Became Mayor of Portland

Mr. Baker and his wife lived in Baker until the theater was well established. Then they returned to Portland where Mr. Baker went on with his work in the business and was elected Mayor of Portland. He was outstanding in this office and well known outside of Oregon. The files of *The Oregonian* are full of pictures of George Baker kissing the stars who came to the city.

At one time Sanford published a little paper called "Stage." It continued for a few months. He gave information about the coming attractions from material sent by the companies. The little paper included ads, some even from national firms such as Royal Baking Powder. Articles were written for each issue on Music, by Frances Streigel Burke and Society, by Mrs. Panting.

This brings up the name of one of Baker's most valued citizens, Mrs. Burke. She accompanied her lawyer husband when he moved to Baker. She was a fine pianist and teacher, having studied in Europe. Her influence on the town was very good. She taught others who became fine artists in their own right. Two of them were Florence French and Gertrude Lachner. Florence herself went to Vienna for study when only eighteen. Mrs. Burke formed the McDowell club for musical study. The club sponsored concerts by local artists, many of them taking place in the little hall in the Carnegie library now used for the Crossroads players. Amateurs gained experience. Mrs. Burke brought some outside musical events to the Opera House.

Another fine musician was Mrs. Jessie Hoskins, who came to Baker after study in Germany. A whole book could be written about Mrs. Hoskins. She was an ebullient little Jewess married to an ebullient little Irishman and she produced a whole town full of good singers. Taking a half hour lesson took about an hour and a half, so much time was taken up with fights with Jake, spankings for the children and talk with passers-by. Sometimes, in the Fall, the whole time would be used to bake Christmas cookies from German recipes.

The Opera House was not only used for plays. It was part of Baker life. High school classes graduated there and there were civic events such as Fourth of July speeches and political meetings. And, of course, many local productions. The Elks' club brought in a professional occasionally who produced plays with local talent.

...And A Cowboy Married a Chorus Girl

The Opera House went on for over thirty years and was never closed for lack of patronage, only by the decline of live theater. It had some early notable movies including "Birth of a Nation."

During the influenza epidemic at the time of the First World War there was an interesting incident. The musical comedy "You're in Love" was set to play at the Opera House but when the company arrived they found the town, even the churches, closed because of the epidemic. The actors were stranded. Sitting in the lobby of the Antlers Hotel waiting for a rescue a Baker County cowboy came along and rescued a chorus girl by marrying her. It would be interesting to know the outcome of this marriage.

When moving pictures and radio finally put an end to traveling live theatre, the Heilners made a moving picture theatre out of the Opera House and changed its name to the Clarick. It saw the birth of the talkies and played first-run movies in the northwest. An era when within a few years the fading stage saw in Baker such productions as "Rio Rita" and not too long thereafter the "talkie" musical by the same name.

The theatre went on in this way for some years but on November 12, 1937, it burned to the ground, a sad ending for a great institution.

Baker Opera House, NE corner of Main and Church streets, built about 1900.

Group of women actors. Back row: Miss McIntyre, Amy C. Haines, Mrs. Swan, Mrs. Horner. Front row: Mrs. Curry, Ada Cleaver, Beulah Bowman.

Carnegie Library, 1909

Alpha Club and the Baker Public Library

In January 1900, some ladies met to form a society. The society was to have a twofold purpose: first, to supply books for a library to study literature, art and issues of the day and, second, to promote the founding of a civic library.

The first members were Emma Faull, Lulu Eppinger, Edith Flynn, Ida May Sage, Grace Goodwin, Maude Palmer, Zetta Bowers, Nea Small, Rofena Miller, Frances Kadish, Belle Dodson and Mary E. Saxton.

The name suggested was "Alpha," meaning beginning. The first President was Mrs. Faull. The program for the first meeting consisted of papers and discussion on the Boer War, that being in the news at the time. Later, programs were on trips around the world, and there was one titled, "The old maid's convention."

The ladies started immediately to earn money to start a library. First, they formed an association to promote the work. Anyone could become a member by subscribing for $5. They gave socials, teas and home talent plays. For one social the price of admission was one book. They secured a nucleus of 250 books. Meeting rooms were donated by William Pollman in the Baker Loan and Trust Building on the corner of Main and Court.

When the City Hall was planned it was decided to allow a room for the library. Over the years a good collection of books was secured. In the Fall of 1905 the library was turned over to the city and became a free public institution supported by a city tax.

Anna Faith Taylor was the first librarian. She stayed as assistant when on March 17, 1906, the library was opened to the public in the City Hall under a trained librarian, Miss Susan Moser. Miss Moser remained for some years after the move into the Carnegie Library.

After the second year in the City Hall it became evident that a library building was needed. The steel financier, Andrew Carnegie, was disposing of some of his wealth by furnishing funds to start libraries and the Baker people appealed to him for help. He agreed and the gift was made on his usual terms. He donated $25,000 and the city was to provide a site and an appropriate sum annually, not less than one-tenth of the amount of his gift, to support the library.

The library was built of native stone and finished inside with native fir. The Alpha Club always met in the basement room used later for the Children's Department and now for Crossroads plays and entertainments.

Lewis and Clark Project

In 1903 the club became involved in another project. Plans were being made in Portland for the Lewis and Clark Fair to be put on in 1905 to celebrate the one-hundredth anniversary of the Lewis and Clark Expedition. In the Spring of 1903 Mrs. Edyth Tozier Wetherred of Portland came to Eastern Oregon to interest women in her project for the Fair. This was to be a Woman's building. This lady would have been a fine addition to the modern Women's Lib movement.

She said, "The men of the Lewis and Clark Fair evidently forgot that there were any women in the state. They should have appointed a woman's board for if they had done so, this work of ours would have been going on for the past year. They forgot that women pay taxes and so we will have to tell them in a good natured way."

The women at the preliminary meeting were enthusiastic about the project. The gathering teemed with enthusiasm. Miss Susan Moore, president, conducted the meeting. Miss Estella Bowen was honored with the position of press agent.

When Mrs. Wetherred returned for her second visit, she found that the Baker women had organized a committee with Miss Moore as president, and Mrs. Ida M. Lachner had gracefully accepted the office of secretary. Ladies on the committee were Mesdames Parker, Goodwin, Johns McClelland, Snow, Bowers, Stuchell, Barton, Brinkley, Bartmess and the Misses Bowen and Helen Stack, principal of the high school.

Mrs. Wetherred had some suggestions to make for the exhibits in the hall. "Among other things," she said, "we must have an exhibit of bottled fruit. Then we must have a pioneers' room, one of those places with a big fireplace and a crane of the biggest pattern. We want a coffee pot that will hold enough coffee so that every pioneer woman who comes can get her coffee. Another idea that occurs to me is to have the farmers' boys send in sheaves of wheat so that each boy will have a personal interest in the Fair.

"Another line is a fine floral exhibit and still another is a collection of ores. Of course, this will be entirely separate from the main mining exhibit but you will find if you ask the men that they will donate some very pretty exhibits.

"We should have a room for different ladies' orders to meet, such as E.O.S., W.O.W., D.A.R., Rebekahs and others."

Mrs. Wetherred then told the story of the Indian maiden Sacajawea who acted as a guide for Lewis and Clark and stated that a monument would be erected to her memory. "The monument will be sculptured by Miss Alice Cooper of Colorado, the lady who designed Colorado's statue of gold for the World's Fair." (This statue of Sacajawea now stands in Portland's Washington Park.)

It was thought fitting by all that the statue should be created by a woman.

Alpha Club Cook Book

The truly big project of the club was the publication of a cook book. It earned for the club more than $2000, a goodly sum in 1904, when it came out. The proceeds of the sale went to the library fund. Members sold the books and fortunately they were not all sold at the time. A few new copies remained in the recent past.

The cook book was dedicated to:

"Those plucky housewives who master their work instead of letting it master them."

It is full of outstanding recipes if the larder happens to hold several dozen eggs, several pounds of butter and a pint or two of rich cream. And, too, the housewife who uses it must know how to judge the heat of an oven by putting in her hand to test it. Seriously, there are many recipes that can easily be used now. Some are for pickles, salad dressings, etc.

The book contained advertisements for businesses now long gone. Here is an example, from the Orange Front Drug Store:

> The Woman
> The Man
> and the Pill

Strangely, it wasn't what you might think now. It advertises a dyspepsia (indigestion) pill for the husband to take after eating the right concoctions in the book.

Other advertisements were:
- *M. Weil and Co. (The best $3.50 shoe in the world)*
- *The Fair Department Store*
- *Crabill Hotel, opposite the Depot*
- *Alexander Clothing Co., (a good, well-tailored suit for $10)*
- *The Baker City Toilet Bazaar (Evenings reserved for Gentlemen).*
- *J. W. Wisdom and Co. Prescriptions a specialty*

The Alpha club continued for many years after the library project was on its own. The members kept up with the times by studying the changing styles in literature and art. They came into modern times in issues of the day, the more complex life after the First World War, the big Depression and finally the Second World War.

An offshoot of the club was the toastmistress division. This became the most important activity of the club. When the library decided to move the Children's department to the lower floor, the Alpha Club moved out of their longtime meeting place. From then on the

club met in the Hotel Baker, sometimes for a luncheon meeting.
A few years later the club ended its long period of usefulness to Baker.

The grand opening of the Hotel Baker took place in August 1929. It was built in 1928-29 with funds from 300 stockholders. The investment never paid off, because the stock market crashed a couple months after the building opened sending the country into a depression that lasted over ten years.

Hotel Warshauer (later, Geiser Grand Hotel) – photo was taken the year the building was built, 1889.

On the back of the photo is "S. B. McCord," possibly his signature. Sirenus B. McCord was Baker City's first mayor.

The Warshauer and the Geiser Grand

The Hotel Warshauer was built and still stands in Baker at Main and Washington streets. It was constructed in the eighties and in early nineteen hundreds was purchased by the Geiser family and re-named the Geiser Grand Hotel.

The structure is of red brick with rounded window construction on the corner topped with a clock tower. Unfortunately, the tower was removed a few years back. [A cupola was added in the 1990's.] The windows on the second floor faced out from the hotel parlor. All hotels of the day had a rather secluded parlor for the ladies so that they need not be subjected to the company of sometimes rough men in the lobby.

There remains to us a little gold cloth hanging, twelve by six inches in size. It is on a little gold rod and trimmed with imitation gold coins.

It seems to have been used on the back of a hotel room door to give the rules and regulations. They were about the same as now except for two of them. Rule 2 was as follows: "Fires in rooms charged extra." This rule seems a little ambiguous but we suppose it refers to fires in stoves for warmth. Rule 6: We will not be responsible for boots and shoes left in the hall. Guests desiring them blacked will please leave with the porter." Hotel guests at that time from eastern cities and from Europe were accustomed to leaving shoes outside their doors and finding them shined in the morning. Baker City was not yet that sophisticated.

The little hanging contains advertising of Baker City merchants. One was for the Arlington Dining Room, under the same management as the hotel. Another was for the White House, one of the fine stores of the time which sold dry goods, fancy goods, boots and shoes. The store was all white inside and out and provided stools for customers to rest themselves. The stools were cushioned with red velvet.

Other advertisers were Ferguson and Warinner, Mining Brokers; M. Bird, Fine Custom Tailoring; Baker City National Bank; Daggett and Donaldson, Druggists and Chemists; Ottenheimer, Baer and Co.; The Clothing and Dry Goods House; Charles St. Louis Jeweler; Hyde, Johns and Olmstead, Attorneys; J. P. Atwood, M.D.; Aaron Fox, Dealer in Boots, Shoes and Gloves, etc.; Art Photographer, A. B. Hooper, Cabinets, $4 per dozen.

Baker City Street Railway at Geiser Grand Hotel

Menu a la Carte

See Daily Bill of Fare for Ready Dishes

OYSTERS

Eastern Transplanted		Shoal Water Bay or Olympia	
Raw on Half Shell	50	Oyster Cocktail	25
Stewed	50	Stewed in Milk	35
Fried	50	Stewed Dry on Toast	40
Pepper Roast	50	Fried	40
Pan Roast	50	Fancy Roast	50
Fancy Roast	60	Pan Roast	40
Raw on Plate	50	Pepper Roast	40
		Raw, per Plate	35
		Oyster Loaves, 50 and 75	

SALADS AND RELISHES

Lobster	40	Combination	30
Crab	35	Celery Salad	20
Shrimp	35	Potato Salad	15
Chicken	40	Pickled Beets	10
Cucumber, Sliced	10	Olives	10
Tomato, Sliced	10	Olives, Stuffed	15
Asparagus	25	Olives, Ripe	15
Celery	25	Mango Peppers	10
Lettuce		Chow-Chow	10
Lettuce with Egg		Radishes	

SHELL FISH

Lobster a la Newberg	60
One-half Fresh Crab, 30; whole	50
Little Neck Clams, Fried	40
Little Neck Clams, Half Shell	35
Little Neck Clams, Steamed	35
Deviled Crab (25 minutes)	50

EGGS AND OMELETTES

Two Poached Eggs on Toast	30	Ham Omelette	35
Two Boiled Eggs	25	Oyster Omelette	60
Two Fried Eggs	25	Spanish Omelette	40
Two Shirred Eggs	25	Pepper Omelette	35
Two Scrambled Eggs	25	Mushroom Omelette	45
Plain Omelette	30	German Pancake	25
		Rum Omelette	40

FISH

Salmon Steak	40	Halibut Steak	40
Choice Salt Mackerel, one-half, 25; whole 40		Fried Tenderloin of Sole	40

STEAKS, CHOPS, ETC.

Plain Steak	30
Sirloin	60
Top Sirloin	50
Sirloin Double	1 00
Tenderloin	70
T-Bone	65
Porterhouse	75
Porterhouse (for two)	1 45
Hamburg Steak	25
Hamburg Steak, with Egg	35
Salisbury Steak	30
Steak a la Tartar, with Egg	35
Mutton Chops (2) 25 (3)	35
Lamb Chops (2) plain	40
Lamb Chops (2) breaded	50
Veal Chops, plain	35
Veal Chops, breaded	40
Veal Cutlets	35
Pork Chops	35
Pork Chops, breaded	40
Ham and (2) Eggs	35
Broiled Ham or Bacon	25
Bacon and (2) Eggs	35
Calf Liver and Bacon	
Breakfast Sausage	35
Weiner Schnitzel	50
Welch Rarebit	50
Spring Chicken (half)	
Golden Buck	60

SAUCES
SERVED WITH MEAT ORDERS

Spanish	15	Mushrooms	20
Tomato	15	Onions	15

Geiser Grand Menu, dated about 1907. This menu is one of several owned by Mrs. Edna Nash and reproduced through her courtesy. One item in another menu was Roast Black Bear from the Geiser ranch.

The Warshauer Was A Proud Hostelry

The Warshauer seems to have been constructed with the backing of Baker City business men. [The Jewish Warshauer brothers of Germany, had the Hotel Warshauer built in 1889.] The proprietor was John R. Burns, a native of Cardiff, Wales, and like most of the Welsh people, a fine musician. The hotel cost a very large sum for those days, $65,000. It was a luxurious hostelry for a small town. It was proud to advertise electric lights, hot and cold water and bath rooms. It contained a fine reception room furnished with writing paper, pens and also newspapers. There was a sample room for drummers (traveling salesmen) and lavatories on the main floor.

Adjoining the office was a dining room, capable of seating 200 people. Any guest was at liberty to inspect the kitchen. "Everything pertaining to it was as clean as can be made."

When Albert Geiser and his family took over the hotel in the early nineteen hundreds it continued as a fine hotel with new additions and improvements. Much entertaining was done there. This writer remembers a beautiful party given as late as 1926, luncheon and bridge on the mezzanine floor. Throughout its early history the dining room was outstanding with shining white tablecloths, large napkins and flowers on all the tables. The black waiters always wore white gloves while serving.

Lobby of Hotel Warshauer, 1890.

SVRy train on trestle. Train is composed of engine, tender #6, baggage and mail car #3, and passenger car #23.

Stuffy Air and Cinders . . . The Sumpter Valley Railway

Since we resided in Baker and the grandparents lived in Canyon City we made many trips back and forth on the old Sumpter Valley Railway.

We packed our valises and grips (remember them?) and the night before departure called, in the early years, Bob Bettner's horse drawn cab and, later on, Manny Fox and his Model T taxi. They were asked to be in good time in the morning to take us to the depot for the train which left at 8 a.m.

Bob or Manny never forgot and when we reached the train we were warmly greeted by Mr. Baird and Mr. Larson. There were usually two cars, one for smoking. We chose the non-smoker. The men in the party always had a chance to smoke a cigar at one of the numerous stops.

Cinders Or Stuffy Air

We chose seats on the shady side and turned over the seat ahead to be more sociable. Then came the big decision, to swelter in the stuffy air or to open the window. If the latter we would soon be covered by cinders as the little engine burned cord wood. At least once on every trip a cinder had to be removed from an eye.

Stops were made at Lockhart and Thompson sidings, at McEwen and at Sumpter, sometimes just to drop off someone or to pick up another passenger. They were often long stops. On one trip my aunt remembered that she had forgotten to turn off the gas under the coffee pot. (Baker had a gas plant then.) There was ample time to call Baker from the Sumpter depot and ask a neighbor to climb in the window and turn off the gas. Since the house didn't burn down, I suppose this was done.

The railroad, when first built, went as far as McEwen then Sumpter, then to Whitney in a year or two as the timber was cut and thinned. Tipton was next, then Austin and finally, great day!, to Prairie City. People were certain that this would be the beginning of a line across the center of the state to Burns or Bend.

We always carried on our trips a large box lunch of fried chicken, ham sandwiches, etc. And on the return included my grandmother's cinnamon buns and sour cream cookies. If we were hungry at the right time we could get off at a stop and have our lunch under the pine trees.

At the end of the line, wherever it might be, we finished our journey on an old-time stage coach. This was not as romantic as on television as I can remember no men with guns or hurdy gurdy ladies.

The narrow guage line was built to bring out logs but also became a useful service to the miners at Sumpter and Bourne. One well-known miner often came to Baker at 4 p.m. He spent most of the night gambling and sometimes took the morning train back. If he overslept and his luck had been good, he could hire an engine to get him back to Sumpter. Real service!

The first trip I can remember on the little train was in 1904 when I was brought here to live with my aunt after my mother died. It was between Christmas and New Year and we had a two-seated sleigh to take us from Canyon City to Austin. There we spent the night. Mrs. Austin, always a good provider, packed us a large lunch which we forgot to take. After a short distance we remembered and returned for it. She said, "It is bad luck to come back." She was right.

We were traveling over the mountain on a very narrow road when around a bend came a six- or eight-horse freight team. Our driver had not heard the bells. Over we went, upside down in the snow, but we were unhurt as the snow was deep and soft. When we got back to Mrs. Austin she said "I told you so." We caught the train anyway at Tipton and how safe and warm it looked.

Last Ride Made in Train in 1922

Almost my last ride on the Sumpter Valley train was an outstanding one. This was 1922.

In Canyon City an organization had been formed, the Whiskey Gulch gang. Its purpose was to celebrate the anniversary of the discovery of gold on Canyon Creek in 1862.

The honor guest was to be Juanita Miller, the daughter of the famous poet, Joaquin Miller. He had lived in Canyon City in the sixties.

The day before the celebration was to begin my aunt and I boarded the train. With us were Anna Gyllenberg (Mrs. Robert Donald) and Louise Pollman (Mrs. G. P. Lilley). On the train was Juanita Miller, a woman of perhaps 35 or 40. She was really turned out for the occasion, a picture in rose color. Rose suit, hat bag and parasol and wearing tennis shoes, which originally white, had been carefully dyed pink. To add to the effect she was surrounded by an aroma of rose geranium.

Miss Miller was gracious and friendly to everyone on the crowded train and I often thought afterward that it must have been a great occasion for her. Her life was always a hard one with the old poet, a hand to mouth existence. Her expenses were paid by the Grant County people and she gave full value for the investment.

Upon arrival in Canyon City she was given a beautiful old fashioned dress to wear and added much to the festivities. She recited her father's poetry and joined in the singing and square dancing. After her return to California we heard of her occasionally and her death occurred only a short time ago.

If the Sumpter Valley Railway could have been preserved intact it would have been one of the great tourist attractions of the United

States. Perhaps we should plan now to keep the Union Pacific tracks.

The present endeavor to bring back some of the little train is a fine idea and I wish all success to them.

[The Sumpter Valley Railway restoration from McEwen depot to Sumpter was completed in 1991.]

Sumpter Valley Railway engine #251 in Boulder Gorge.
This is the bridge that replaced Red Bridge.

About the Author

Helen Biggs Rand (1898-1985) came from Eastern Oregon pioneer stock, as did her husband, Irving Rand. So it probably came as a surprise to no one who knew her that Helen chose to write about the history of Eastern Oregon.

Helen's maternal grandmother, Mabel Hazeltine Biggs, was the daughter of George Irving and Emeline Hazeltine, who were settlers of Canyon City in 1862. Both George and brother, Martin M. Hazeltine, who settled in Baker City in 1884, were famous photographers before coming to Eastern Oregon from California.

Helen's father, John W. Biggs, was a Burns lawyer, who married Mabel Hazeltine of Canyon City. Mabel died when Helen was just six years old. She was raised in Baker City by her maternal aunt, Edith Hazeltine Clifford, wife of attorney and former Circuit Court Judge Morton Clifford. Helen graduated from Baker High School in 1916 and from a Los Angeles school of library science in 1923. She worked as a librarian in Portland, until she married lawyer Irving Rand in 1926.

Irving's father, John Langdon Rand of Baker City, was married to Edith Packwood, daughter of Baker County pioneers of 1862 William H. and Johanna Packwood. Before coming to Eastern Oregon, William was the youngest member of Oregon's Constitutional Convention of 1857. And Irving's father became Chief Justice of the Oregon Supreme Court.

Besides "Gold, Jade, and Elegance" (1974), Helen compiled and edited in the same year "One Hundred Years of St. Stephen's Episcopal Church, Baker City, Oregon, 1873-1973". In 1981, Helen wrote "Whiskey Gulch" about early Grant County history based mostly on the 1862-1863 correspondence between her maternal grandparents, when George was getting settled in Canyon City and Emeline was still in Northern California. Shortly before she died, Helen wrote " Recollections of Burns, Oregon," based on the stories her father told.

Helen and Irving had one child, Mary Rand Ballantyne, who lives in Boise, Idaho. Mary says of her mother, "She had a great love for all that country (Eastern Oregon) and a great curiosity about people and history." — *Biographical sketch of Helen B. Rand by Gary Dielman*

Gold, Jade and Elegance

www.ingramcontent.com/pod-product-compliance
Lightning Source LLC
Chambersburg PA
CBHW020659300426
44112CB00007B/457